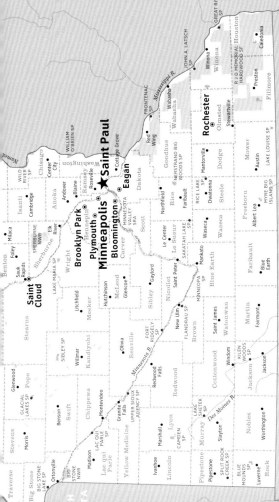

WISCONSIN

Norton

WILLIAM
O'BRIEN SP

WILD
RIVER
SP

Chisago

Center
City

★ Saint Paul

Roseville

Cottage Grove

Washington

Ramsey
Blaine

Andover

Anoka

Cambridge

Isanti

Benton

Sauk
Rapids

Foley

Milaca

SHERBURNE
NWR

Wright

Elk
River

Hennepin

Brooklyn Park

Plymouth

Minneapolis

Bloomington

Eagan

Dakota

MINNESOTA
VALLEY
SRA

Scott

Carver

Saint
Cloud

Stearns

LAKE MARIA SP

Litchfield

Meeker

McLeod

Hutchinson

Glencoe

Sibley

Gaylord

Le Sueur

Le Center

Nicollet

Saint Peter

SAKATAH LAKE
SP

New Ulm

FLANDRAU SP

Brown

FORT
RIDGELY
SP

Mankato

Blue Earth

MINNEOPA
SP

Waseca

Faribault

Northfield

Rice

Goodhue

Red
Wing

FRONTENAC
SP

Wabasha

Wabasha

Mississippi R.

JOHN A LATSCH
SP

Winona

Winona

GREAT RIV...
SP

R J D MEMORIAL Houston
HARDWOOD SF

Caledonia

Preston

Fillmore

Rochester

Olmsted

Stewartville

Dodge

Mantorville

Mower

Austin

LAKE LOUISE SP

Steele

Owatonna

RICE LAKE
SP

NERSTRAND BIG
WOODS SP

Faribault

Albert Lea

Freeborn

MYRE BIG
ISLAND SP

Blue
Earth

Watonwan

Saint James

Martin

Fairmont

Glacial
Lakes SP

GLACIAL
LAKES SP

Glenwood

Pope

Benson

Swift

Stevens

Morris

Chippewa

Montevideo

LAC QUI
PARLE SP

Granite
Falls

UPPER SIOUX
AGENCY SP

Kandiyohi

Willmar

SIBLEY SP

Olivia

Renville

Redwood
Falls

Redwood

Minnesota R.

LAKE
SHETEK
SP

Murray

Slayton

CAMDEN
SP

Lyon

Marshall

Lincoln

Ivanhoe

Madison

Lac qui
Parle

Yellow Medicine

Luc qui Parle
NWR

Ortonville

BIG
STONE
LAKE SP

BIG STONE
NWR

Traverse

Big Stone

SOUTH
DAKOTA

Pipestone

Pipestone

SPLIT ROCK
CREEK SP

BLUE
MOUNDS
SP

Rock

Luverne

Nobles

Worthington

Cottonwood

Windom

WILEN
WOODS
SP

Jackson

Jackson

Des Moines R.

IOWA

American Birding Association

Field Guide to Birds of Minnesota

Laura Erickson

PHOTOGRAPHS BY
Brian E. Small
AND OTHERS

Scott & Nix, Inc.
NEW YORK

A SCOTT & NIX EDITION

COPYRIGHT © 2016, 2021 BY SCOTT & NIX, INC.
ALL RIGHTS RESERVED.

PUBLISHED BY SCOTT & NIX, INC.
150 W 28TH ST, STE 1900
NEW YORK, NY 10001
SCOTTANDNIX.COM

FIRST EDITION 2016
SECOND PRINTING 2021

ISBN 978-1-935622-59-8

AMERICAN BIRDING ASSOCIATION®
AND ITS LOGO ARE REGISTERED TRADEMARKS OF
THE AMERICAN BIRDING ASSOCIATION, INC.
ALL RIGHTS RESERVED.

AMERICAN BIRDING ASSOCIATION, INC.
800-850-2473
ABA.ORG

SCOTT & NIX, INC. BOOKS
ARE DISTRIBUTED TO THE TRADE BY:

INDEPENDENT PUBLISHERS GROUP (IPG)
814 NORTH FRANKLIN STREET
CHICAGO, IL 60610
800-888-4741
IPGBOOK.COM

THIS BOOK IS PRINTED ON FSC® CERTIFIED PAPERS,
WHICH ASSURES IT WAS MADE FROM WELL MANAGED
FORESTS AND OTHER CONTROLLED SOURCES.

PRINTED IN SOUTH KOREA

Contents

The American Birding Association inspires all people to enjoy and protect wild birds.

The ABA represents the North American birding community and supports birders through publications, conferences, workshops, events, partnerships, and networks.

The ABA's education programs promote birding skills, ornithological knowledge, and the development of and implementation of a conservation ethic.

The ABA encourages birders to apply their skills to help conserve birds and their habitats, and we represent the interests of birders in planning and legislative arenas.

We welcome all birders as members.

THE AMERICAN BIRDING ASSOCIATION
CODE OF ETHICS

Everyone who enjoys birds and birding must always respect wildlife, its environment, and the rights of others. In any conflict of interest between birds and birders, the welfare of the birds and their environment comes first.

CODE OF BIRDING ETHICS

1. Promote the welfare of birds and their environment.

   1(a) Support the protection of important bird habitat.

   1(b) To avoid stressing birds or exposing them to danger, exercise restraint and caution during observation, photography, sound recording, or filming.

Limit the use of recordings and other methods of attracting birds, and never use such methods in heavily birded areas, or for attracting any species that is Threatened, Endangered, or of Special Concern, or is rare in your local area; Keep well back from nests and nesting colonies, roosts, display areas, and important feeding sites. In such sensitive areas, if there is a need for extended observation, photography, filming, or recording, try to use a blind or hide, and take advantage of natural cover.

Use artificial light sparingly for filming or photography, especially for close-ups.

1(c) Before advertising the presence of a rare bird, evaluate the potential for disturbance to the bird, its surroundings, and other people in the area, and proceed only if access can be controlled, disturbance minimized, and permission has been obtained from private land-owners. The sites of rare nesting birds should be divulged only to the proper conservation authorities.

1(d) Stay on roads, trails, and paths where they exist; otherwise keep habitat disturbance to a minimum.

2. Respect the law, and the rights of others.

2(a) Do not enter private property without the owner's explicit permission.

2(b) Follow all laws, rules, and regulations governing use of roads and public areas, both at home and abroad.

2(c) Practice common courtesy in contacts with other people. Your exemplary behavior will generate goodwill with birders and non-birders alike.

3. Ensure that feeders, nest structures, and other artificial bird environments are safe.

3(a) Keep dispensers, water, and food clean, and free of decay or disease. It is important to feed birds continually during harsh weather.

3(b) Maintain and clean nest structures regularly.

3(c) If you are attracting birds to an area, ensure the birds are not exposed to predation from cats and other domestic animals, or dangers posed by artificial hazards.

4. Group birding, whether organized or impromptu, requires special care.

Each individual in the group, in addition to the obligations spelled out in Items 1 and 2, has responsibilities as a Group Member.

4(a) Respect the interests, rights, and skills of fellow birders, as well as people participating in other legitimate outdoor activities. Freely share your knowledge and experience, except where code 1(c) applies. Be especially helpful to beginning birders.

4(b) If you witness unethical birding behavior, assess the situation, and intervene if you think it prudent. When interceding, inform the person(s) of the inappropriate action, and attempt, within reason, to have it stopped. If the behavior continues, document it, and notify appropriate individuals or organizations.

Group Leader Responsibilities [amateur and professional trips and tours].

4(c) Be an exemplary ethical role model for the group. Teach through word and example.

4(d) Keep groups to a size that limits impact on the environment, and does not interfere with others using the same area.

4(e) Ensure everyone in the group knows of and practices this code.

4(f) Learn and inform the group of any special circumstances applicable to the areas being visited (e.g. no tape recorders allowed).

4(g) Acknowledge that professional tour companies bear a special responsibility to place the welfare of birds and the benefits of public knowledge ahead of the company's commercial interests. Ideally, leaders should keep track of tour sightings, document unusual occurrences, and submit records to appropriate organizations.

Everyone who enjoys birds and birding must always respect wildlife, its environment, and the rights of others. The ABA Code of Ethics should be read, followed, and shared by all birders.

Please follow this code and distribute and teach it to others.

The American Birding Association's Code of Birding Ethics may be freely reproduced for distribution/dissemination. An electronic version may be found at aba.org/about/ethics.

Foreword

Minnesota is simply a great state for birding. Here, you're blessed with a diversity of habitats ranging from tallgrass prairie to the North Shore, and the wilderness of the Boundary Waters to the teeming Twin Cities, each with its own set of birds. Add in four distinct seasons and a prime position along the Central Flyway and it's easy to see why so many Minnesotans enjoy watching birds.

Like all the guides in this series, this book can help you do whatever you want with birding. Perhaps you enjoy birds a few days a year in your yard or local park and just want to know a little more about them. Or maybe you want to dive deeper and really get familiar with the hundreds of amazing birds that call Minnesota home for part or all of each year. Our aim is to meet you where you are and give you useful, reliable information and insight into birds and birding.

Author Laura Erickson is the perfect guide for those wanting to explore Minnesota's birds. She brings a wealth of knowledge of her subjects but most important, has that inspiring combination of enthusiasm and a sincere desire to share that marks the best teachers. The gorgeous photography by Brian Small and others will not only aid your identifications—it will inspire you to get out and see more of these beautiful and fascinating creatures for yourself.

I invite you to visit the American Birding Association website (aba.org), where you'll find a wealth of free resources and ways to connect with the birding community that will also help you get the most from your birding in Minnesota and beyond. Please consider becoming an ABA member yourself—one of the best parts of birding is joining a community of fun, passionate people.

Now get on out there! Enjoy this book. Enjoy Minnesota. And most of all, enjoy birding!

Good birding,

Jeffrey A. Gordon

Jeffrey A. Gordon, *President*
American Birding Association

Birds in Minnesota

Minnesota has a reputation as an inhospitable, mosquito- and blackfly-infested wilderness in summer and a frozen wasteland in winter. If you're a warbler, though, it's the right place to raise young. If you're a northern owl, it's a great winter getaway. And if you're a birder, it's a heavenly place to enjoy a lot of birds.

The twelfth largest state encompasses dense coniferous and hardwood forests and remnants of wide-open tallgrass prairie. Lake Superior, the largest lake in the world, forms the state's northeastern boundary, and Lake of the Woods pushes Minnesota's border farther north than any other of the Lower 48. In addition to the 11,842 lakes, 69,200 miles of rivers and streams meander through the state, among them the mighty Mississippi, which rises in Itasca State Park and works its way down to form our southeastern border.

Thanks to the state's size and wealth of habitats, 316 bird species occur regularly in Minnesota; 39 more are "casual" (seen in 3–8 of the past 10 years), and 81 are "accidental" (not seen more than twice in the past 10 years). At least five birders have seen more than 400 species in the state, and at least two have seen over 300 here in a single year. In addition to life lists and state lists, many birders keep lists of the birds they've seen in their county, city, favorite birding spots, and backyard. No one should go through life listlessly.

The Common Loon is an excellent state bird for this "land of 10,000 lakes."

But our birds are much more than simple check marks on a list. Loon calls mingling with the howling of wolves under flashing northern lights; the eerie booming of Greater Prairie-Chickens as dawn silhouettes an Upland Sandpiper; Northern Cardinals, Blue Jays, and Pine Grosbeaks adding vivid color to a snow-covered pine; a Great Gray Owl's forbidding yellow eyes meeting ours across a boggy field: these are just some of the magical moments to be relished while birding Minnesota.

When the temperature plunges to double digits below zero, Black-capped Chickadees call and sing as the winter sun rises, warming our hearts even if they can't protect us from frostbite. In spring, dozens of birds—Winter Wrens, Hermit Thrushes, Veeries—sing from the woodlands. On summer afternoons, as the mercury inches towards 100, long after other birds have quieted down for the season, Red-eyed Vireos sing away, just because singing is what they do. No matter where we are and no matter what time of year, Minnesota is a great place to enjoy birds.

Found in almost every bit of forest in the state, the Red-eyed Vireo sings from May well into August.

Birds in This Guide

Anyone, from seasoned birders to people who have never picked up binoculars or a bird book, can encounter a rare bird in the backyard, but this book would be unwieldy if it were to include every one of the 436 species on the Minnesota list. Instead, this guide introduces 300 of the birds we're most likely to encounter birding on our own, including some "casual" species that, when they do appear, often turn up in someone's yard. A few "regular" species that are unpredictable or especially hard to find have been excluded, but a few rare "regular" species are described in the entry for a similar, more common species. As our interest in birds grows, or as we start searching for rarities or focusing more closely on such diverse groups as shorebirds, gulls, warblers, or sparrows, we will be drawn to other, more comprehensive field guides.

The birds in this guide are organized roughly in what is called "taxonomic order," the sequence used in the American Ornithologists' Union *Check-list of North and Middle American Birds* (AOU). That sequence is intended to illustrate current scientific understanding of the relationships among species — relationships that may not always be intuitive.

For example, the AOU sequence places ducks quite a distance from coots and from loons: these three may be superficially similar on the water, but research has determined that they are only distantly related genetically. Hawks and owls both have talons, but they aren't close relatives. DNA analysis has shown that falcons are much more closely related to parrots and songbirds than they are to hawks. Crows and ravens are widely separated genetically from blackbirds.

With practice, you will learn how to find birds in this guide quickly without using the index. At the start, though, it is easiest to remember one general rule: Songbirds are found in the second half of the book; the wide variety of other birds makes up the first half.

Within families or smaller groups, such as geese, if one species is much more abundant, widespread, and likely to be encountered than the others, that one is placed first in this guide, regardless of its position in the AOU sequence.

Habitats

Every bird is adapted to one or more particular habitats in a particular range. We see Greater Prairie-Chickens only in extensive treeless grasslands—a habitat that happens to be one of the few in which we would virtually never see Black-capped Chickadees. Prairie-chickens are habitat specialists, while chickadees are generalists.

Red-winged Blackbirds range across the entire state; Yellow-headed Blackbirds are hard to find in the northeastern quarter. In marshes where both are found, the Yellow-headeds usually stick to the areas of deeper water.

Though they can be found in just about every city, town, and farm in Minnesota, Rock Pigeons, House Sparrows, and European Starlings are not well adapted to the northern forests, and so none have ever been seen on the Isabella Christmas Bird Count, which takes place in a rural area entirely within the Superior National Forest.

Important as it is to associate birds with their preferred habitats, we should also remember that every single warbler traveling between its breeding area in Canadian wilderness and its wintering area in the tropics must cross Interstate 90 twice a year, along with plenty of other unfamiliar and even inappropriate habitats. Most of the hawks that migrate over Hawk

The Greater Prairie-Chicken is an iconic species of extensive grassland with few or no trees visible on the horizon.

Ridge each fall—birds that Duluthians can see from their backyards—never nest or winter anywhere near Duluth. Observing birds through the seasons, in our own backyards and farther afield, helps us piece together this wonderful puzzle.

And there is always more to learn. Even researchers who are intimately familiar with birds are still learning. In 2015, scientists used high-tech tracking to discover that during the nesting season, male Wood Thrushes spend the night far from their nests, often in habitats never before thought to be useful to them. Even though birding is fun and easy, it's a never-ending learning process.

Bird Sounds

Describing with human words the sounds birds produce is tricky. Birds don't have lips, their tongue is entirely different from ours, and instead of a simple larynx, they have a complex "song box" called a syrinx. Great Horned Owls make sounds that are easy for most of us to imitate with our speaking voices, and a handful of birds, such as Black-capped Chickadees and White-throated Sparrows, have a clear whistle that many people can imitate well, but for the most part, bird songs and calls are very hard to adequately describe. And to complicate things more, some species show a lot of individual variation in their songs. Some mimic a wide variety of sounds, including songs and calls of other birds. And most birds have a variety of calls in addition to their territorial and breeding song.

Our two meadowlarks look almost identical, but their songs make them easy to tell apart; this Eastern Meadowlark has a simpler whistled tune.

In this guide, we focus primarily on the most commonly heard song of each species. To describe each one, we have tried to choose a mnemonic, a memory aid, that captures the rhythm and a bit of the tone quality and energy level of the song phrases. Unfortunately, there is no way to learn bird songs except by actually hearing them. Watching a bird singing away is an ideal way to commit the song to memory. When you are out birding, try to track down as many singers as possible, both to confirm the ones you're familiar with and to learn new ones. Listening to recordings at home while reading our descriptions may help jog your memory later when you hear a bird in the field.

The Parts of a Bird

Like humans and other mammals, birds are warm-blooded vertebrates, but their bodies are quite different. The upper leg bone (the femur), the knee joint, and most of the lower leg bone are completely hidden by feathers on birds; what looks like a backwards knee is actually the ankle, and what looks like their lower leg corresponds to the foot bones in our bodies. But it would sound odd, even if it is anatomically accurate, to say that a Great Blue Heron has long feet, especially because the elongated tarsus functions exactly as our legs do.

In this guide, we try to use intuitive words to describe those parts of bird bodies most important in identifying them. After all, even the most astute ornithologists ignored comparative anatomy when they named the Sharp-shinned and Rough-legged Hawks for features of what look to us like the birds' lower legs. We could use the technical term "ear coverts" for the part of the face that the Gray-cheeked Thrush was named for, but "cheek" works just as well. Asia's Eyebrowed Thrush is named for a feature technically and accurately called the supercilium but intuitively called the eyebrow.

PARTS OF A PINTAIL
This Northern Pintail shows the parts of the
body visible on swimming loons, grebes,
ducks, and many other water birds.

PARTS OF A GULL
Gulls, shorebirds, and many
other long-winged species
show essentially the same
body features as this
breeding adult Herring Gull.

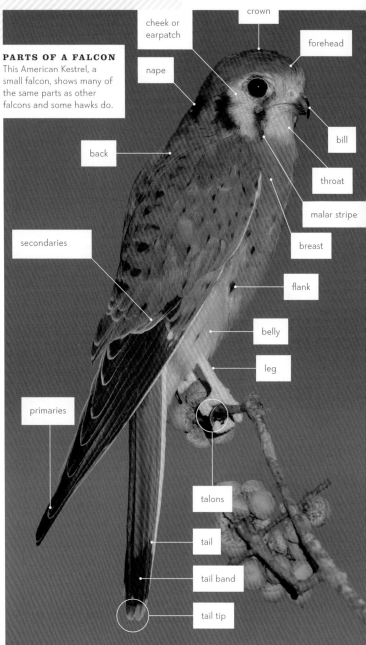

PARTS OF A FALCON
This American Kestrel, a small falcon, shows many of the same parts as other falcons and some hawks do.

crown

cheek or earpatch

forehead

nape

bill

back

throat

malar stripe

breast

secondaries

flank

belly

leg

primaries

talons

tail

tail band

tail tip

**PARTS OF A
SONGBIRD**
Blue Jays are among
the most beautifully
and complexly marked
of our songbirds.

crown

eyebrow

eye line

crest

nape

throat

back

breast

primaries

leg

toe

tail

FLIGHT FEATHERS   The flight feathers are the long, sturdy feathers of the wings and tail. The flight feathers of the wing are divided into primaries (the nine or ten feathers farthest from the body, attached to the hand bones) and secondaries (a variable number of slightly shorter feathers closer to the body, attached to the arm bones). Smaller feathers called coverts overlap the bases of the long wing and tail feathers, smoothing the contour of the wings and tail.

FACE AND HEAD MARKINGS Owls, with their forward-facing eyes, have facial discs of stiff feathers that, like a satellite dish, gather sounds and focus them to the ears. The facial discs of this Boreal Owl (top) are pale. Some owls also have feather tufts positioned on the head like horns or a cat's ears, as on this Great Horned Owl (bottom). Its facial discs are orange.

The area directly between the eye and bill, or right above that area, is called the lore; the lore is yellow on this White-throated Sparrow (left). A line all the way through or behind the eye is the eye line, which is black on this bird. The top of its head, the crown, is white with black borders. The eyebrow, the line above the eye, is white on this Red-eyed Vireo (right). Its eye line is blackish, and its gray crown is bordered with black.

When eye rings are connected to lores, the result is spectacles. They're white on this Blue-headed Vireo (left). The feathers covering a bird's ear are called the ear coverts or, more simply, the cheek. The cheek is orange on this Cape May Warbler. The sides of its neck are yellow.

WING MARKINGS Some birds have one or two contrasting lines, or wing bars, on the folded wing, a mark that can be very helpful in identification. This Yellow-throated Vireo (above) has two prominent wing bars (and yellow spectacles).

This Ruby-crowned Kinglet (below) has one prominent wing bar edged with black. The male's red crown feathers can be raised in display or hidden beneath the duller feathers of the rest of the crown.

Some birds have two wing bars connected with white to produce a wing patch, as in this adult male Magnolia Warbler (above).

The bold patch of contrasting color on the upper wing of a displaying Red-winged Blackbird (below) is called an epaulet.

Some birds, such as this Yellow-rumped Warbler (above), have colorful patches on the sides just below the wings.

TAIL FEATHERS The terminal band, a contrasting bar at the tip of the tail, is yellow on this Cedar Waxwing (below).

This Magnolia Warbler's (above) tail has a broad black terminal band, accentuated by the broad white band above it.

This American Kestrel (below) has a conspicuous dark tail band, each feather ending in white; when the tail is closed, those white tips form a narrow terminal band.

In some species, the outer tail feathers, or the edges of the outer tail feathers, are of a contrasting color. The white outer tail feathers of a Dark-eyed Junco (above) are even more conspicuous when the bird flies.

Tail feathers may be rounded or pointed at their tips. In some birds, such as this Pine Siskin (below), the central tail feathers are shorter than the others, creating a conspicuous notch.

This Northern Cardinal's tail feathers are all the same length, making the tail tip square rather than notched.

Northern Harriers have white upper tail coverts.

TAIL COVERTS Feathers covering the base of the tail above or beneath, hiding the down feathers and the bases of the flight feathers, are called coverts; the coverts sometimes form a contrastingly colored patch.

Palm Warblers have yellow undertail coverts.

RUMP A contrasting patch on the lower back, just ahead of the upper tail coverts, is the rump, the feature the Yellow-rumped Warbler (below) is named for.

Mastering Bird Identification

Field guides are short on plot, and so are seldom read from cover to cover the way other kinds of books are. Even if you choose not to give this guide a close reading, keep it at hand and thumb through the species entries often. Your growing awareness of the possibilities and increasing familiarity with the book's organization will help you identify new birds more quickly and easily.

Birds are functionally illiterate and haven't read any bird books, so they often do unexpected things or show up in unexpected places; virtually every "accidental" or "casual" bird on Minnesota's list appeared here unexpectedly, and many common birds show up in unexpected locations now and then. Almost every new birder comes across a rare bird or two not long after starting birding. Even so, the vast majority—almost all—of the birds we see are exactly where the bird books say they should be, doing exactly what the bird books say they should do.

Some species have striking and unique plumage characteristics that make their identification simple and straightforward; others are more challenging. The most important identifying features may be subtle and hard to see, the bird may be positioned with parts of its body obscured by vegetation, or it

Red-breasted Nuthatches are typically found in coniferous woods of the north but pay no mind to what is "typical," often appearing in backyards away from forests, and often in the south, too.

may take off before we have seen enough. The more birds we do identify, the more quickly we figure out the next one.

You can build your "life list" (all the birds you've seen in the wild) most quickly by birding with experts on field trips and at birding festivals, and the tips your more experienced companions provide will be invaluable. But you will become most proficient at identification when you painstakingly figure out the birds on your own. Combining the two—attending field trips, but taking plenty of time to bird by yourself in your own backyard and other places—is the fastest way to learn birds well.

Take the time to study the common birds you already know. At the migration overlook at Hawk Ridge, many people who know their backyard robins and jays have trouble recognizing these same species flying overhead in flocks. When your backyard robin takes off, keep your eyes on it to notice how it whips its pointed wings back in flight. You can't usually see the red breast from below, but the pure white lower belly and undertail coverts stand out against the dark breast and tail. From below, flying Blue Jays may not look blue at all. But they have a distinctively slow and direct flight, rounded wings, and a long straight tail.

Take a second look at the markings of those and other common birds, looking for wing bars, eye rings, eye lines, eyebrow stripes, or conspicuous rump patches. Study the body shape, focusing especially on the size and shape of the bill and how long the wings and tail are.

Size is far less important than other features. Ravens are much larger than crows, and Herring Gulls much larger than Ring-billed Gulls, but unless they're flying side by side, you should key in on elements of shape, relative bulk, and movement.

When you see birds in magazines or online, try to identify them before you read the captions. Quiz yourself with birding apps, or cut up an old field guide to make flash cards. Quizzes can refresh your memory of, say, warblers or shorebirds after a long winter, or help you learn the birds anticipated on an upcoming trip to a new area. Quizzes on birding apps have the added bonus of songs and calls.

Where to Bird in Minnesota

Birding spots everywhere in the state can be great year round, but birders searching for specialties and spectacles concentrate at some of the best sites at specific times of the year.

AFTON STATE PARK, WASHINGTON CO.
Spring and summer Grasshopper and Henslow's Sparrows, meadowlarks, and other grassland birds.

AGASSIZ NATIONAL WILDLIFE REFUGE, MARSHALL CO.
Spring through fall Franklin's Gull (one of world's largest nesting colonies), Red-necked Grebe, and other water and grassland species.

BEAVER CREEK STATE PARK, HOUSTON CO.
Spring and summer Southern specialties such as Acadian Flycatcher, Cerulean Warbler, and Louisiana Waterthrush.

BELTRAMI ISLAND STATE FOREST AND LAKE OF THE WOODS, LAKE OF THE WOODS CO.
Winter and early summer Northern and bog specialties such as Northern Hawk Owl and Connecticut Warbler.

Handsome little Henslow's Sparrows are hard to find almost anywhere in the state, but are fairly reliably seen every June at Afton State Park.

Gorgeous Blue Grosbeaks often turn up at Blue Mounds State Park in summer.

BIG STONE NATIONAL WILDLIFE REFUGE, LAC QUI PARLE CO.
Spring through fall   Western Grebe, American White Pelican, and other water birds and western specialties.

BLUE MOUNDS STATE PARK, ROCK CO.
Spring through fall   Grassland and western species such as Western Kingbird and Blue Grosbeak, and migrating Swainson's Hawk and occasionally Lark Bunting.

CROOKSTON, POLK CO.
Spring   Greater Prairie-Chicken, Marbled Godwit, Upland Sandpiper, and other grassland species.

DULUTH, ST. LOUIS CO.
Fall through spring   Raptor migration, Glaucous, Thayer's, and other winter gulls, large warbler migration.

FELTON PRAIRIE, CLAY CO.
Summer   Chestnut-collared Longspur and other prairie birds.

GRAND MARAIS, COOK CO.
Spring and fall   Uncommon migrants such as Harlequin and Long-tailed Ducks and Townsend's Solitaire. Many out-of-range birds such as King Eider, Anna's Hummingbird, Fork-tailed Flycatcher, and Fieldfare have made an appearance here.

ITASCA STATE PARK, CLEARWATER CO.
Summer   About twenty nesting warbler species, including Connecticut and Golden-winged Warblers.

LAKE BRONSON STATE PARK AND TWIN LAKES WILDLIFE MANAGEMENT AREA, KITTSON CO.

Spring and fall   Grassland and water birds such as Eared Grebe, Gray Partridge, Sharp-tailed Grouse, and Franklin's Gull, and even an occasional Swainson's Hawk.

MCGREGOR MARSH AND RICE LAKE NATIONAL WILDLIFE REFUGE, AITKIN CO.

Summer   Yellow Rail and Nelson's Sparrow. Winter: Great Gray Owl.

MURPHY-HANREHAN PARK, DAKOTA CO.

Summer   Southern specialties including Acadian Flycatcher and Blue-winged, Cerulean, and Hooded Warblers.

PIPESTONE MONUMENT, PIPESTONE CO.

Spring through fall   Both cuckoos, Dickcissel, and Orchard Oriole breed. Unusual western birds such as Bell's Vireo, Rock Wren, and Brewer's Sparrow are rarely seen on migration.

ROTHSAY WILDLIFE MANAGEMENT AREA, WILKIN CO.

Fall and winter   Greater Prairie-Chicken and Short-eared Owl are regular. Exceptionally rare Prairie Falcons are seen here more than any other place in the state, and Smith's Longspurs pass through in mid-October.

SAX-ZIM BOG, ST. LOUIS CO.

All year   Great Gray and Northern Hawk Owls, Black-backed Woodpecker, Canada Jay, Boreal Chickadee.

TWO HARBORS, LAKE CO.

Winter   Bohemian Waxwing and winter owls.

Resources

Kim Eckert, the first birder to see 400 species in Minnesota, shares his intimate knowledge of birding places in the state in his indispensable *A Birder's Guide to Minnesota*. Out of print but still available in libraries, this is the best single reference for a comprehensive overview of the state's habitats and best birding spots.

Audubon Minnesota's birding trail maps also provide an excellent overview of some great places. Bob Janssen and Carrol Henderson's *Birds of Minnesota State Parks* is a wonderful introduction to the birds you can see in these jewels of our landscape.

A fine resource for finding birds in the state, guaranteed to stay up to date, is the Cornell Lab of Ornithology's eBird website (ebird.org). Click "Explore Data," then "Explore a Region," and enter "Minnesota" or a county name for hotspot maps and complete bird lists. If you click on "Bar Charts," you can see how frequent each species is at any time of year. Clicking on the species name will give you even more information, including a map of recent sightings. The eBird app lets you enter the birds you see in the field and provides additional resources for the traveling birder.

The Minnesota Ornithologists' Union promotes birding in the state with its journal, *The Loon*, and a newsletter, *Minnesota Birding*. The MOU's "Minnesota Birding Weekend" trips provide exceptional opportunities to bird some of the best areas in the state in the company of great birders who are happy to share their knowledge. The Minnesota Ornithologists' Union Facebook group provides information about current sightings. The MOU website (moumn.org) also provides a way to report birds and keep track of your Minnesota list.

This field guide will help you identify most of the birds you're likely to encounter, but you'll want to consult a more compre-hensive guide to identify other species or to figure out unusual plumages of some common species, such as Red-tailed Hawks and Herring Gulls. Two excellent choices are the *National Geographic Field Guide to the Birds of North America* by Jon Dunn and Jonathan Alderfer (National Geographic, 2011) and *The Sibley Guide to Birds* by David Sibley (Knopf, 2014). Both titles are also available as apps that include songs and calls for almost every species.

American Birding Association

Field Guide to Birds
of Minnesota

Canada Goose

Branta canadensis

L 29.9–43.3″ | **WS** 50–67″

The quintessential goose can be found just about anywhere
spring through fall, near open water in winter. The Giant
Canada Goose is the main subspecies that breeds here, joined in
much of the year by other subspecies varying widely in size and
shape; all have a black neck and face, white cheek and throat,
and white undertail. Rarer species sometimes feed and fly with
Canadas. Flocks fly in V formation, as do many other birds, such
as cormorants, pelicans, cranes, and gulls. Many different calls
and honks used in different contexts.

Note the long,
slender neck
and long bill.

Can scrunch down its neck
to appear as short as a
Cackling's. Note the
somewhat long, slender bill.

Cackling Goose

Branta hutchinsii

L 21-29" | **WS** 48-54"

This "miniature Canada Goose" of the tundra, long thought to
be a subspecies of the Canada Goose, was named a separate
species in 2004. Uncommon but increasing here on migration,
often in mixed flocks with Canadas, it's often seen from Hawk
Ridge in fall. It is much smaller than most Canadas, but some
Canada subspecies are almost as small. The Cackling's neck is
shorter and thicker than on virtually all Canadas. As the name
suggests, it gives high-pitched squeaks and yelps; more typical
honks are higher-pitched than the Canada's.

Like tiny Canada Goose with
short neck and stubby bill.

Snow Goose

Anser caerulescens

L 27-33" | **WS** 54"

This large, sturdy goose can be seen anywhere in spring, with
fewest in the northeast and most in the southwest; thousands
gather in farm fields and wetlands. Regularly seen migrating
along Lake Superior in fall. "Snow Goose" describes the white
form usually seen here. Darker "Blue Goose" adult shares white
head, pink legs and feet, and pink bill with a dark "grin patch."
Young blue form can be mistaken for extremely rare Brant.
When a boisterous flock takes off, the noise is deafening. Most
calls are high-pitched, single honk-like notes; a lower call
sounds like a Great Blue Heron's *kronk*.

Black is limited to primary
wing feathers, unlike other
large white birds.

"Grin patch" on
bill. Black feathers
often hidden on
folded wings.

Ross's Goose

Anser rossii

L 22.5-25" | **WS** 44.8"

The Snow Goose, like the Canada, has a tiny counterpart. Fairly rare but increasing, this "mini Snow" is barely larger than a farm duck. Like the Cackling Goose, Ross's is seen only in migration, often in mixed flocks with Snows, mostly in the west and also, in fall, from Hawk Ridge. Much smaller than Snow, with shorter neck; at close range, note its stubby bill without a "grin patch." A distant flock, whether grazing or flying, can be hard to identify without Snow Geese for comparison. Less vocal than Snow Goose, but has a quiet, high-pitched call and a soft, cranky, heron-like note.

Smaller than Snow Goose, with no "grin patch" on tiny bill.

Absence of grin patch visible only at close range.

Greater White-fronted Goose

Anser albifrons

L 25-31.8" | **WS** 53.1"

In spring, scrutinize swimming, grazing, or flying geese to pick out an occasional "specklebelly" among the more abundant Canada and Snow Geese. Sightings are spottier in fall, more restricted to migration pathways such as river valleys and the Duluth shoreline. Dark speckling on the belly and white at the base of the bill are most noticeable in adults. Orange legs are usually brighter than the pink legs of adult Snow Geese. White patch on face is smaller than the white on typical blue-form Snow Geese. Gives high-pitched two- or three-noted calls and lower, crankier single tones.

White at the base of the pale bill.

In flight, the speckled belly can be conspicuous.

Tundra Swan

Cygnus columbianus

L 47–58″ | **WS** 66″

This northern swan appears during migration and, rarely, winter. Formerly called Whistling Swan for its high-pitched calls, it's locally common on wild rice paddies and along the Mississippi, where thousands once gathered every November; current high counts are usually in the hundreds. Yellow between eye and bill can be hard to see, and many individuals lack it. Note the slightly concave bill compared to the even slope of Trumpeters. Young bird in dusky plumage may have a pink bill in fall. Migrating flocks often give clear, high-pitched musical notes with some wavering tremolos.

Curve of back often steeper than on Trumpeter; usually yellow near eye. Bill tapers toward eye; upper bill concave.

Trumpeter Swan

Cygnus buccinator

L 54–62" | **WS** 80"

This swan, wiped out here by the late 1800s, was reintroduced in the 1980s; currently numbers more than 2,400. Pairs or small groups can be found locally spring through fall. Some remain through winter where water is open, especially in Pioneer Park in Monticello. Careful study of Trumpeter Swans in summer and winter helps when you're trying to identify Tundra Swans on migration. Larger than the Tundra Swan, but size hard to judge even in mixed groups. Any yellow near the eyes or bill excludes this species. Young Trumpeters keep dusky plumage over winter; the bill may be partly pale but is always black at the base. If you spot a swan with an orange bill with a black knob, it's an exotic Mute Swan. Calls, lower-pitched than Tundra Swan calls, sound as if produced by a trumpet with a mute.

Back forms an even, shallow curve; upper bill slopes evenly; black at base of upper bill seems to engulf the eye.

Dusky young Trumpeter always has black at base of bill.

Swans have no black feathers. Note long neck, black bill, and big black feet. Many wear neck bands.

Wood Duck

Aix sponsa

L 18.5–21.25" | **WS** 26–29"

This extravagantly beautiful duck nests in natural cavities and nest boxes, and often perches in trees. In low light, note the helmeted shape and, in flight, the squared tail. Teardrop-shaped eye ring on female's soft gray face is diagnostic. Wood Ducks are common throughout, from ice-out in spring through fall, but extremely rare in winter. Females give a high-pitched *er-RUK, er-RUK, er-RUK* call. In flight and some other situations, they can be very loud, but utter a softer version of the call almost constantly when leading chicks. Males give a comical high-pitched, rising *Jeeeeeep!*

Male unmistakable. Note the "fingered" white throat patch.

Female has teardrop-shaped white eye ring and shaggy head.

Mallard

Anas platyrhynchos

L 22″ | **WS** 34″

Abundant year-round. Near Lake Superior, found mostly in
harbors and parks. Male's bill yellow, female's orange with dark
central splotching. Male's head iridescent except in summer,
when it resembles female. Both sexes show two white borders
on blue wing patch. This is the parent species of most domesticated ducks, and it hybridizes with many other species. Over
generations, feral farm ducks come to resemble wild Mallards
except for larger size and, on males, wider neck band. Calls
include a variety of quacks and grunts. Females give a series of
quacks descending in pitch, like derisive laughter.

Male with yellow bill,
shiny head, curly
black tail feathers.

Female with dark-marked
orange bill; white edges
on wing patch.

Gadwall

Mareca strepera

L 18.1–22.4" | **WS** 33"

Large, sturdy duck with fine, delicate markings. Note male's gray head, dark body, and black rear end. Females look like female Mallards but have a subtler eye line, especially in front of the eye, and a steeper forehead. Both sexes have a white wing patch that shows in flight or when the wings are opened just right. Seen throughout the state during migration; breeds most commonly in western and central regions. Males give a low, soft *burp* call that seems quiet but can carry quite a distance over water. Females don't call often; their quacks are a bit lower than those of Mallards.

Male with black rump; no white except often hidden wing patch.

Female with steep forehead, subtle eye line, delicate bill.

American Wigeon

Mareca americana

L 20" | **WS** 33"

Nicknamed "baldpate" for the male's pale forehead, this long-bodied, tiny-billed duck migrates throughout, breeding mostly in the north. Dabbles for aquatic plants and sometimes associates with diving ducks to steal deep-water plants from them. Also grazes on land. Flies in dense flocks; male shows a white forewing. Optimistic birders search flocks for the extremely rare Eurasian Wigeon, males of which are rusty-headed with a creamy buff forehead. Male American Wigeon produce a two- or three-noted whistle, usually preceded by a soft, sometimes inaudible lower note. Females give a low, wavering quack.

Male with whitish "pate," white before black tail, tiny bill.

Female has dark around eye, small gray bill with black tip.

American Black Duck

Anas rubripes

L 21-23" | **WS** 34.5-37.5"

This typical East Coast duck is adapted to salt and brackish water. Widespread here, but far less common than Mallard; always rare in the southwest. Common on Lake Superior even in winter. Frequently hybridizes with Mallards; hybrids can have traits of both. Most Black Ducks here probably have some Mallard genes. Male's solid greenish-yellow bill has a black tip; soft gray face contrasts with dark crown and body. Female's green bill can be flecked with black. Dark blue wing patch bordered by black. Calls include varied quacks and grunts. Females give a series of quacks descending in pitch.

Male darker than female Mallard; black-tipped yellow bill. Any green on a Black Duck's head reveals Mallard genes.

Blue-winged Teal

Spatula discors

L 15" | **WS** 23"

This puddle duck has a long, low-slung profile. Large white crescent between eye and bill on males; also note speckling on body feathers and white separating brown side from black tail. In both sexes, large powder-blue wing patches, hidden on folded wings, are conspicuous in flight (also seen in Northern Shovelers). Green wing patch similar to that on Green-winged Teal, but bill proportionally longer. In spring, a stunning but extremely rare Cinnamon Teal may show up with Blue-wingeds in temporary ponds in the west. Males give rapid, high-pitched chattering calls; females utter squeaky quacks.

Male has large white face crescent and long, slender bill.

Female has long, slender dark bill and noticeable eye line.

Northern Shoveler

Spatula clypeata

L 18″ | **WS** 30″

This puddle duck, seen in migration anywhere, breeds mostly
in the western half. Feeds in tight bunches, hunkering low
in the water. Male has green head with tiny golden eye, dark
back and tail, and rusty sides and belly set off fore and aft by
gleaming white. Large soft blue wing patch as in Blue-winged
Teal (usually seen only in flight) is grayer in females. Swimming
females look like Mallards with an oversized bill. Females
produce a quacky chatter. Males make a single or double-
noted beeping sound, or combine several beeping notes into
a distinctive chatter.

Pairs often swim very close
together, as do feeding flocks.
The front half of the very long
bill widens dramatically.

Northern Pintail

Anas acuta

L 17.5-20" | **WS** 31"

This large duck, seen throughout on migration, breeds mostly in the west. Muted plumage, long neck, and slender, dark gray bill in both sexes. Male's gray sides and lower nape appear solid at a distance, but are finely etched; his back feathers are long and pointed. The long, tapering neck stripe reaches the back of the brown head; creamy flanks balance the snow-white breast. The male's tail is the pièce de résistance on an exquisite duck, and a comical adornment when he's tipping up. The female's quack is hoarser than a female Mallard's. Males produce a soft, whistled whoop.

Black edges on gray bill; long tail, white neck stripe.

Note slender female's subtle eye line and narrow dark bill.

Green-winged Teal

Anas crecca

L 12.2-15.3″ | **WS** 20.4-23.2″

This handsome and tiny duck is a fairly common migrant throughout the state, favoring edges of shallow, muddy ponds; it's present more regularly in summer than the few breeding records would suggest. Rusty head with large green patch enclosing the eye and ear is striking in good light. Creamy patch under the tail in both sexes. Green wing patch, hidden when wing is folded, also found in Blue-winged. Females shorter-bodied, with a tinier bill than other teal. The female's quack is shriller and weaker than other ducks'. The male's whistles can be confused with spring peepers.

Note vertical white stripe on side, creamy undertail.

Note female's small bill and creamy patch under tail.

Canvasback

Aythya valisineria

L 21″ | **WS** 33″

Both the Canvasback and Redhead can be found throughout on migration, often together; both breed mostly in the west and central areas. Canvasbacks can be very common on the Mississippi in fall. The even slope from the crown to the tip of the solid black bill is distinctive in both sexes. Male's back and sides are very whitish and unstreaked. Note the female's head shape and the contrast of the dark head, neck, and breast with pale back and sides. Like other diving ducks, females give growling quacks. Males give haunting *hooooah* calls, often punctuated with squeaky calls and quacks.

"Ski slope" from crown to bill tip, unstreaked white back.

Female with black bill and subtle whitish eye ring and eye line.

Redhead

Aythya americana

L 19″ | **WS** 29″

This handsome duck often associates with the slightly larger Canvasback during migration throughout; both breed mostly in the prairie pothole areas in the west and central parts of the state. The Redhead male's back and sides are silvery gray with delicate etching; his bill is pale blue with a black tip. The female's head and bill shape, shorter neck, overall dark plumage, and bluish-gray bill with black tip distinguish her from the Canvasback. She often has a subtle eye ring but no eye line. Female gives a soft, low *kurr kurr* quack. Male gives a low, rather gull-like *whaaa whaaa*.

Male has gray back and bluish bill with a black tip.

Female all dark with pale eye ring; black-tipped gray bill.

Ring-necked Duck

Aythya collaris

L 17" | **WS** 25"

Our most widespread diving duck from spring through fall often associates with other ducks. It might have been better named the Ring-billed Duck: the male's bill is ringed with white at the face (most noticeable in breeding season) and near the black tip. His whitish sides meet the black back in an elegant curve. Both sexes have a noticeably peaked head. Females have a whitish eye ring, gray cheeks contrasting with dark cap, and pale at the base of the bill, usually less well defined than on female scaup. Ring-necked Ducks are seldom heard, but give grunting quacks and whistles when courting.

White vertical stripe at edge of breast is conspicuous.

Female with peaked head, dark bill with pale ring near tip.

Greater Scaup

Aythya marila

L 19″ | **WS** 30″

Hunters call scaup "bluebills"; bill is blue or gray. The Greater
Scaup, seen most often in deep water, is very similar to the
Lesser. Male of both has whitish-gray sides and back between
very dark front and back ends, and female is brown with a pale
patch at base of bill. In flight, the white wing stripe of Greaters
extends farther onto the primary wing feathers; this is hard to
see in some light. The head shape of all ducks changes with the
bird's activity, but the Greater Scaup's head averages rounder
than the Lesser's; if it shows a peak at all, it's close to the front.
Seldom heard here.

Male's rounded head usually green but may appear purple.

Female brown with whitish face patch, round head.

Lesser Scaup

Aythya affinis

L 17" | **WS** 29"

This "bluebill," almost identical to the Greater Scaup, is seen during migration throughout, often in large flocks with other diving ducks; it breeds in the northwest. It is less restricted to deep water than the Greater Scaup, but the two overlap even in this. The male's iridescent head often appears blue, but can look green in many lighting conditions. The head of both sexes usually shows a subtle but noticeable peak at the rear of the crown, much less conspicuous than in the Ring-necked Duck. Female scaup never have a ringed bill, unlike female Ring-neckeds. Seldom heard in Minnesota.

The head usually shows a peak near the back of the crown.

Female dark except for pale at base of bill; head subtly peaked.

Harlequin Duck

Histrionicus histrionicus

L 12-21" | **WS** 22-26"

Reports of a Harlequin Duck make the state rare bird alert. It breeds in western mountains and winters on rocky coasts; most reports here, from late fall through early spring, are on Lake Superior. Note the male's horizontal and vertical white stripes and large white face patch. Female has small clean white oval and smaller, duskier patches on face, which can stand out even in poor lighting. The Harlequin is endangered in Canada and declining in the U.S. Rapid-fire chattering quacks are high-pitched and squeaky, giving Harlequins the nickname "sea mice," but they seldom call here.

Note adult male's unique dark and white pattern.

Female shows oval ear patch and diffuse patches near bill.

Surf Scoter

Melanitta perspicillata

L 23" | **WS** 30"

This sea duck, nicknamed the "skunkhead," appears on migration in small flocks, sometimes with other scoters, on Lake Superior, rarely elsewhere. All three scoters are chunky and big-headed, with mostly dark plumage and oversized bill. They usually stay far from shore, and flocks fly in a line. To identify from a distance, key in on the shape and position of any white patches. Adult male Surf's bill and head striking and unique; young male usually shows a bit of white on nape. Female similar to female Harlequin but with a larger bill; Harlequins don't associate with scoters. Seldom heard here.

Adult male unique. Young have white on nape by late winter.

Female has thicker body and bill than Harlequin Duck.

White-winged Scoter

Melanitta fusca

L 21" | **WS** 31"

Scoters are found primarily during migration on large lakes,
especially Lake Superior, usually far out on the water; they're
very rare elsewhere. The male White-winged Scoter's squiggly
white eye ring and oversized black and yellowish bill are useful
marks. The face patches of the female are better defined than
those of female Surf Scoters or Harlequin Ducks. The white
wing patch is often hidden when birds are swimming, but is
very useful when scoters are seen in flight, even in mixed flocks
at a distance. Like other scoters, is seldom heard in Minnesota.

White eye squiggle,
large bill with black
base, pale tip.

White patches on face; white
wing patch is usually hidden.

Black Scoter

Melanitta americana

L 19" | **WS** 33"

This rare migrant is mostly found way out on Lake Superior and other deep lakes. The male is all black except for a smooth yellow knob at the base of the bill. The female is patterned like a non-breeding male Ruddy Duck, with a distinctive pale cheek that contrasts with the black cap; both species tend to hold their tail up. The Black Scoter's cheek patch is duskier, helpful only after you've studied both species. Fortunately, both species tend to be seen in flocks with their own kind, so if in doubt, look at nearby birds. Scoters are seldom heard here.

Yellow at the base of the bill on all-black adult male.

The female has a dusky cheek contrasting with her black cap.

Long-tailed Duck

Clangula hyemalis

L 15-23″ | **WS** 28″

Flocks of this small but sturdy, chatty duck sometimes appear, especially on Lake Superior, from late fall through mid-spring. The dark and light plumage is variable, but all birds have some white on the face and dark on the lower breast. The wings are always entirely dark, though the white back feathers of a swimming male can conceal the wings. Male has a very long tail. Persistent vocalizers; their grunting, quacking, and yodeling calls carry well and can be heard from shore when the wind and waves are quiet. Adult males start giving their melodious *ooooh-owl-a-loop* breeding calls in February.

Male has stubby pink and black bill, long tail, black breast.

Female and immature brown and white, some white on face.

Bufflehead

Bucephala albeola

L 14" | **WS** 21"

This tiny duck is a common migrant throughout the state, and is a rare, local breeder, mostly in the northwest. Often called "butterball" by duck hunters, it has a relatively large head: the scientific name means "buffalo head." Males appear black and white from a distance or in poor light, but the head has a dark purple or green sheen in good light. Observant birders may see the striking bubblegum-pink feet when a Bufflehead dives or preens. Both sexes have a tiny bill. The clean oval ear patch on the female's dark head can be seen even in poor light. Buffleheads are usually silent.

Male with dark back and face; white breast, sides, head patch.

Female is darkest on head and back; clean white ear patch.

Common Goldeneye

Bucephala clangula

L 18″ | **WS** 32″

This big-headed diving duck nests in the north, migrates throughout, and overwinters locally. Adult male has white oval between eye and bill and mostly white sides. Female has reddish-brown head and grayish body. Any yellow on female's bill limited to tip. In late winter and spring, male performs a head-jerking display. Rarely, a flock is joined by a Barrow's Goldeneye, which has a tinier bill. Male Barrow's has a crescent face patch and more black on back and sides; female has an all-yellow bill. Wings make a loud whistling sound. Calls include raspy whistles and low rattles.

Adult male has mostly white sides and round face patch.

Female has a rich brown head and grayish brown body.

Hooded Merganser

Lophodytes cucullatus

L 17" | **WS** 25"

Mergansers have a longer, narrower bill than other ducks. The common but secretive Hooded breeds throughout, often in Wood Duck boxes. One of the earliest arrivals in spring, it keeps to wooded ponds more than other mergansers. When crest is lowered, male may be mistaken for the much whiter Bufflehead, but has chestnut sides and two black vertical marks between breast and side. Female has a thicker, shaggier crest than other mergansers. When females are on eggs, males molt into female-like plumage. Displaying male gives a deep croak: *baaa waaaaa*. Female croaks softly.

Male has brown sides with black marks, black edging on crest.

Overall brown, with thick, shaggy crest and very dull bill.

Common Merganser

Mergus merganser

L 24" | **WS** 33"

The Common Merganser migrates throughout, overwinters locally, and nests in cavities mostly in the north; families are often seen in the Boundary Waters. The low-slung, long shape is loon-like, but male is much whiter, female browner, and both have a red bill as if wearing lipstick. Male has a round, iridescent greenish head. Female has a shaggy, "wind-blown" crest like the Red-breasted Merganser; the female Common's head meets the neck in a more defined line, and she has a white throat patch. Displaying male produces faint bell-like or banjo-plunking calls. Both sexes also make low croaking sounds.

Male has bright red bill and pure white breast and sides.

Female has white throat, clean line between head and neck.

Red-breasted Merganser

Mergus serrator

L 22" | **WS** 27"

This common migrant with a low-slung profile breeds in the
forested north, migrates throughout, and overwinters locally.
Often seen in large flocks, it is easily distinguished from loons
by the shaggy crest of both male and female, which gives it a
funky, windblown look. The long, thin reddish bill doesn't have
the bright "lipstick" appearance of the Common Merganser.
Male has a white neck band above the rusty breast, and is
grayer overall than the Common. The female has a less defined
line between head and neck, and lacks the white throat of the
female Common. Both sexes seldom vocalize.

Male with long bill,
shaggy crest, white neck
ring, rusty breast.

Female with shaggy crest,
dusky neck and throat.

Ruddy Duck

Oxyura jamaicensis

L 15" | **WS** 23"

This thick-necked, wide-billed duck breeds mostly in the west and central areas and migrates throughout, though it is rare in the forested north. Often holds stiff tail feathers erect. Breeding male's rich chestnut feathers, bright white cheek, and large blue bill "pop" on a roadside ditch or pond. Non-breeding male dark gray with white cheek; can be mistaken for female Black Scoter, but the Ruddy's cheek patch is much whiter. Female is patterned like male but duskier, with a dark line across her cheek patch. Displaying male makes muffled popping sounds. Female gives a low, nasal quack and a high squeak.

Breeding male has bright white cheek, blue bill.

Female and young have a dusky line across the pale cheek.

Ring-necked Pheasant

Phasianus colchicus

L 24″ | **WS** 28″

This large game bird, introduced to North America from Asia, is a permanent resident, especially in agricultural areas and overgrown fields of southern and central Minnesota; a tiny population in the Duluth area was wiped out by harsh winters in the 1980s. Male's red face, white neck ring, and long tail make him unmistakable. Brown female has a longer neck, much longer tail, and plainer underparts than grouse. Occasionally roosts in trees. Male "crows" year round. Listen for the excited *Augh! Augh!* followed by a whirr of strong wingbeats. Most other sounds heard only at close range.

Male has conspicuous red face, white neck ring, long tail.

Female soft brown with very long tail.

Northern Bobwhite

Colinus virginianus

L 10″ | **WS** 12.9-14.9″

This native quail, listed as a common bird in steep decline throughout its range, was fairly common in southeastern Minnesota up to the 1920s, but probably wasn't normally found in the state before game farms and game management practices were started in the 1800s. Every year there are sightings here and there, anywhere in the state, but virtually all are of birds escaped from game farms and retriever training clubs. A small population centered in Houston Co. may be established. Escapees from game farms can be surprisingly conspicuous thanks to the strong, clear, whistled *Bobwhite!*

The male's dark and white face pattern is distinctive.

Note female's brown and buffy facial pattern.

Gray Partridge

Perdix perdix

L 12–13″ | **WS** 21–22″

This softly colored, plump game bird, introduced to North America from Europe, has become a permanent resident of southern and western Minnesota, where it prefers agricultural areas to grasslands. Its cryptic colors and quiet ways make it tricky to find; it's usually chanced upon at dawn and dusk along roadsides in farm country. In both sexes, the face is less strongly patterned than in the Northern Bobwhite, and the rusty side stripes are distinctive. Lucky birders are sometimes close enough to hear the weird, scratchy *kuta, kut, kut, kut* call.

Both sexes gray with rusty markings, distinctly striped sides.

Ruffed Grouse

Bonasa umbellus

L 16–20″ | **WS** 20–25″

This permanent resident of the forested north and east is usually gray; a small number are rusty. The tail has a pale-edged black terminal band; a displaying male struts with the tail fanned and black neck feathers erect in a ruff. The scruffy crest is distinctive even in low light. Often seen at dawn and dusk in winter, on roadsides or in aspen trees. "Drumming" male produces soft, muffled thuds that start slow and speed up, as if someone dropped a bowling ball in the woods. Both sexes make various cackles and other sounds. When flushed, the wingbeats are startlingly loud.

Often sits in aspens in winter. The shaggy crest gives the head a pointed look; black tail band often visible.

Spruce Grouse
Canachites canadensis

L 15-16″ | **WS** 22″

This dark grouse of the far north has a round head with no crest. The all-dark tail, shaped like a Ruffed's, can be edged with brown. Male is much darker than Ruffed or Sharp-tailed. Female is colder gray, with pale flecking on the back. Found in spruce rather than aspen forests; where habitats mix, can be seen in same area as Ruffed. Birders look for Spruce Grouse in winter at the northern end of Lake County Highway 2, where they pick up grit on the roadside. Spruce Grouse feed and roost in spruce trees, usually well hidden in thick branches. Wings are noisy on takeoff.

Much darker and rounder-headed than Ruffed Grouse. Red skin above the male's eye is visible at close range.

Sharp-tailed Grouse

Tympanuchus phasianellus

L 16-19" | **WS** 26"

This resident of grasslands in the northern half of the state is far rarer now than historically. The tail is short and pointed. The male's orange-yellow eyebrow is also seen in Greater Prairie-Chicken, which is much more restricted in range and has a broad tail. In late winter and spring, males gather on leks; locations may be found on eBird. To watch display, arrive before dawn and stay until the birds leave. At first light, the erect white triangular tail moving in the grass is distinctive. Displaying male chatters and stomps his feet. Usually silent off the lek except for occasional clucks.

Finely marked, round-headed, with pointed tail.

Displaying bird inflates neck sacs and yellow eyebrows.

Greater Prairie-Chicken

Tympanuchus cupido

L 17″ | **WS** 28″

Our rarest grouse, a species of Special Concern, is a permanent resident of some west-central prairie areas. Reintroductions continue in the effort to maintain the dwindling population. Requires far more extensive grasslands than does Sharp-tailed Grouse. Evenly barred underparts and limited range distinguish from other grouse. Birders visit observation blinds managed by the DNR and Nature Conservancy to see displays in April and May. Displaying male gives a wondrously eerie "booming" call, like blowing air over a bottle, *whhoooo-doo-doo*, as well as various cackles. Mostly quiet away from the lek.

Air sacs are orange; neck feathers form a headdress.

Air sacs can be deflated and the headdress feathers lowered.

Wild Turkey

Meleagris gallopavo

L 42" | **WS** 53"

This splendid game bird was probably never established in the state before its successful introduction in 1971; now it's a permanent resident in the south and central areas, and appears occasionally in the north. It's omnivorous, found in many habitats, and often seen in trees as well as on the ground. Driving by at the speed limit, birders can confuse a distant turkey, alone or in a flock, with geese, Sandhill Cranes, or even deer. Displaying male is impressive. Turkey gobbles can be heard from a good distance, but to count one on your list, you must be sure you're not hearing farm turkeys or a hunter using a turkey call.

Dark and huge; head appears oddly tiny.

Sometimes displays in the open.

Common Loon

Gavia immer

L 31" | **WS** 46"

Our state bird breeds on clear lakes in northern and central areas, and migrates throughout. Adult has large head with bulging forehead, intricately etched neck band, and black back and sides checkered with white. Virtually every loon seen here is a Common, but Pacific Loon (with a subtle chin strap) or the extremely rare Yellow-billed Loon (large bill entirely pale) may appear in fall on large lakes. The long "wail" call draws family members closer. Laugh-like "tremolo" is given in flight or when an eagle flies over; if you hear it, scan the skies. "Yodel" calls are given by males, usually at night.

Breeding adult's back black and white; bill black.

In fall has pale throat and breast; bill can be mostly pale.

Red-throated Loon

Gavia stellata

L 24″ | **WS** 43″

Our smallest loon is rare but regular, usually seen on western Lake Superior in late May and early June, often from Park Point in Duluth. Adults in non-breeding plumage and immature birds have more delicate speckling on the back and more white on the face than Commons. The slender bill has a slightly curved lower mandible. It's easy to misidentify a distant immature cormorant as this loon; both species share the pale throat and neck and long, low-slung body, and both tilt the head up. The cormorant always has a straight yellowish bill with a hooked tip. Seldom heard in the state.

Delicate speckling on back, more white on face than Common.

In breeding plumage, the only loon with a red throat.

Pied-billed Grebe

Podilymbus podiceps

L 13.5" | **WS** 21"

Grebes swim and dive like ducks, and often compress their feathers and expel air from their body to sink like a submarine. Our most abundant grebe is found from spring through fall throughout the state on all but the shallowest bodies of water. It's small and stocky, with fluffy white feathers at the rump end where a tail ought to be. Breeding Pied-billed Grebe has a wonderfully bizarre call, revving up with several loud *kuk kuk* notes before breaking into a long series of *Kowp! Kowp! Kowp!* yells, each seemingly punctuated with an exclamation point.

Breeding adult has black and white bill and black throat.

Non-breeding bird has fluffy white rear and thick bill.

Horned Grebe

Podiceps auritus

L 13″ | **WS** 23.5″

This red-eyed diving bird, designated Endangered in the state, breeds in the Boundary Waters and northwest, and appears on migration throughout, mostly on larger lakes. It may dive or slowly submerge. Spring and summer adult can raise and lower "horns" at will; the golden feathers follow the contours of the head, and are always higher than the cheek. White-cheeked non-breeding bird has white on throat; Red-necked Grebe has white cheeks in breeding plumage when entire neck is red. Quiet on migration; breeding bird gives a nasal, descending *aaarrrhhh* and various whiny notes.

Golden "horns" above cheek; red eyes, rusty neck and sides.

Non-breeding bird has white cheeks and throat.

Red-necked Grebe

Podiceps grisegena

L 17-22" | **WS** 24-35"

This handsome dark-eyed grebe is a common breeder on some northern and central lakes; it's easy to find at Agassiz National Wildlife Refuge, and often seen in late April and May on Lake Superior. In spring, may be mistaken for a Horned Grebe still in winter plumage; note red neck and dark sides. Non-breeding adult is duskier than breeding bird; the bill is yellowish, and the cheeks aren't as white as Horned Grebe but whiter than Eared Grebe. Male and female plumages are identical. Seldom heard except during the breeding season, when it makes a long series of whinnies, honks, and other strange sounds.

Breeding bird's white cheeks contrast with red throat.

Non-breeding bird duskier than Horned, bulkier than Eared.

Eared Grebe

Podiceps nigricollis

L 11.8-13.7" | **WS** 20.4-21.6"

The most abundant grebe in the world, found on almost every continent, is rare here. It nests locally in small numbers in the west and is a rare migrant throughout, least likely in the northeast. Wherever it does show up, it seems to gravitate to sewage ponds. All-dark breeding adult is tiny and delicate, with golden feathers fanning out across the black cheek. Non-breeding bird duskier than Horned. In all plumages has a tiny bill and red eye. When courting and nesting, gives various squeaky calls, often including rising two-noted calls; seldom heard during migration and winter.

Golden feathers radiate across black cheek; dark overall.

Non-breeding Eared Grebe smaller and duskier than Horned.

Western Grebe

Aechmophorus occidentalis

L 25.5" | **WS** 33"

An elegant study in black and white, the lithe Western Grebe breeds in the west and appears, rarely, on migration anywhere. The slender bill is as long as the head. Displaying pairs bob heads and suddenly break into a synchronized dance on the water. Clark's Grebe, once thought to be the same species, is a rare migrant west; breeding records here may all involve hybrid pairings with Western. In Clark's, the dark crown stops short of the eye, which is bordered with white; the yellow bill has little or no dark edging. Western call is a *kick-ki-dick*, most often heard during the breeding season.

Dark crown extends to the eye; yellowish bill is dusky along ridges. Black and white pattern in all plumages except downy young.

Double-crested Cormorant

Nannopterum auritum

L 31.5″ | **WS** 46.5″

This relative of pelicans is shaped like a goose in flight and like a loon in the water. It has bare orange skin at the base of the long, slightly hooked bill. Adult has solid black plumage; immature is brown with a pale breast. After swimming, it stands on a pier, rock, or other structure, revealing its large webbed feet and holding its wings outstretched to dry its wing feathers. It breeds in colonies throughout; the stick nests can be conspicuous in dead trees. The population is increasing. Adult is usually silent except for an occasional pig-like grunt. Young at nest squeals.

Young bird dusky overall with yellow hooked bill.

Adult is black with orange at base of bil

American White Pelican

Pelecanus erythrorhynchos

L 49.2-64.9″   **WS** 88.1-114″

This species of Special Concern breeds mostly in the west, but on migration may appear anywhere. When facing away while swimming, it can be confused with a swan; when it turns, the massive bill and throat pouch are unmistakable. In flight, the extremely short tail accentuates the length of the wings. The primary and secondary flight feathers are black, obvious in flight but hard to see when the wings are folded. At rest or in flight, the stretchable pouch skin fits rather tightly along the bill. Adults are silent except for occasional quiet grunts. Begging chicks make loud, whining grunts.

olded wings show
ttle or no black; bill
onger than neck.

Black along most of the trailing edge of the wings.

American Bittern
Botaurus lentiginosus

L 28.5" | **WS** 36"

This stocky, brown-streaked heron is a master of cryptic coloration. It often raises its bill, the vertical neck stripes camouflaged by surrounding marsh vegetation. It breeds mostly in the north and central areas, and can be seen in migration throughout. The blackish mark along the throat is distinctive. In flight, the wings seem more pointed than in other herons. The dark flight feathers contrast with the lighter inner wing. The distinctive pumping call, usually given at twilight or in the night, starts with several gulping sounds and then an *ooon-ka-choonk!* Sometimes gives a guttural squawk in flight.

Black throat mark is distinctive; bill usually held upward.

Head may droop; inner wing lighter than outer primaries.

Least Bittern

Ixobrychus exilis

L 12″ | **WS** 16″

This tiny, secretive heron breeds in all but the northeast. The throat and breast are striped with white rather than shades of brown as in the much more massive American Bittern, and the body is mostly patches of solid colors rather than a cryptic blend. The cap and back are black in adult males, brown in females. Because of its rusty sides and black crown, the Green Heron may be mistaken for this much rarer species. The Least Bittern's guttural *coo-coo-coo* is deeper than the similar *cu-cu-cu-cu* of the Black-billed Cuckoo, which sometimes calls from brushy stands near the same marshes.

Paler than Green Heron, less cryptic than American Bittern.

Great Blue Heron

Ardea herodias

L 38-54" | **WS** 66-79"

Our largest heron breeds and migrates throughout; may remain into early winter. It moves slowly and grabs prey with a lightning-fast jab. In flight, pulls the muscular neck and massive bill toward center of gravity; stiff wings held in curve on both upstroke and downstroke (cranes hold wings flatter). Solitary except when nesting; large stick nests in bare trees reveal a colony. Adult has loose nuptial plumes on breast and back. Fledgling, full-sized when it leaves the nest, is more dully colored than adult. When disturbed, it makes a grunting *kronk!* Nestling noisily clacks bill.

Adult has loose nuptial plumes and black at bend of wing.

In flight, bill and neck are drawn in; legs trail behind.

Great Egret

Ardea alba

L 40″ | **WS** 54″

This heron, more svelte than the larger Great Blue, breeds in the south and west, and may be seen anywhere in late summer and spring migration, least frequently in the northeast. It's frequently observed along interstates near the Twin Cities. When hunkered down, it seems rather small. In flight, it pulls in its snaky neck and heavy bill. The smaller, chunky Cattle Egret also has a yellow bill and black legs. A white heron with a dark bill or light legs may be a rare Snowy Egret or Little Blue Heron. Egrets croak, squeak, and give other harsh calls that seem out of keeping for such an elegant bird.

Our only large white heron with orange bill and black legs.

Distinctive heron flight, with neck pulled in.

Snowy Egret

Egretta thula

L 24″ | **WS** 39″

This dainty, pure-white egret is a rare migrant, mostly in the south and west, with three breeding records in the state. The bill is needle-like and solid black (but juveniles may have a mostly yellow bill); legs are black (but juveniles may have yellowish or black and yellow legs), and the feet are always bright yellow. This egret often runs erratically, sometimes spreading its wings, while chasing prey. Young of the much rarer Little Blue Herons are also white; their blue-gray bill has a black tip. Snowy Egrets are usually quiet except when nesting.

Leg and bill color are important in identifying white herons. Note the "golden slippers" and the needle-like black bill.

Cattle Egret

Bubulcus ibis

L 18-22" | **WS** 39.3"

This small heron is extremely rare in the state but can pop up anywhere, most often in fields and pastures. Body and neck can seem thick until it stretches its neck to appear longer. Adults have a yellow bill; the bill on juveniles is dark but thicker than a Snowy Egret's. Leg color is variable: yellow, reddish, or black. Cattle Egrets are extremely sociable, but vagrants may appear here all alone. Breeding birds (extremely rare in the state) can have soft brownish plumes on crown, back, and breast. May give raspy *rick-rack* calls when roosting in a group.

Only the Great Egret has a similar bold orange bill; the Cattle Egret is tinier, thicker-bodied, and shorter-necked.

Green Heron

Butorides virescens

L 17″ | **WS** 26″

This fairly common small heron breeds throughout except in
the far northeast. It's bigger, thicker-bodied, and darker than
the Least Bittern and more colorful than the American Bittern;
unlike either bittern, it usually holds its bill horizontal or
slightly downward. At water's edge or perched on a branch, it
can hold stock-still for minutes, and so is often overlooked. Its
size and steady, regular wing beats make it seem crow-like in
flight, but orange feet are often visible behind. Its loud *skeow!*
call is louder, sharper, and higher-pitched than a night-heron's.

Dark cap, some rufous on
face and sides, greenish
wings and back. Legs and
feet can be orange-
yellow or greenish yellow.

Black-crowned Night-Heron

Nycticorax nycticorax

L 24" | **WS** 45.5"

Shaped like the more common Green Heron, this larger heron breeds locally in the south and west. Adult is black and white with a red eye. Bittern-like immature usually holds its bill at or below the horizontal and has a hunched-over posture. Roosts quietly in trees during the day, so is often overlooked. The far rarer Yellow-crowned Night-Heron has similar immature plumage; Black-crowned usually has a thinner, bicolored bill, not all-black. Documentation of Yellow-crowned usually requires photos. Gives a barking *quork!* deeper than the *skeow!* of a Green Heron.

Adult is clean black and white, with a blood-red eye.

Immature holds bicolored bill level or lower.

White-faced Ibis

Plegadis chihi

L 18.1-22″ | **WS** 37″

This large, all-dark wader with a downcurved bill is very rare
in the state, but sometimes appears in a wet field or pond. If the
face is clearly bordered with white feathers behind the eyes and
under the chin, adults can be identified with certainty. Reddish
facial skin or red eye also distinctive. Otherwise it is very
similar to the even rarer Glossy Ibis. Clear photographs may
be necessary to identify it to species; most dark ibis are simply
called "unidentified *Plegadis* species." Neither ibis is heard
often in the state, but may sometimes give quiet, nasal moans.

This adult has
white face, red
eye, and reddish
facial skin.

Red eye and
reddish face
confirm this as
White-faced.

Turkey Vulture

Cathartes aura

L 41″ | **WS** 68.5″

This common and increasing scavenger breeds throughout the state from November to March, most rarely in the far northwest. Wingspan approaches that of Bald Eagle, but it weighs less than half as much. In the air, it seems all wings and tail, soaring with wings in a shallow V. Forewings, body, and tail are blackish brown, flight feathers silvery gray. Adult's tiny head is red; immature's is black. Wing beats labored; it seldom flaps more than 10 times in a row. Extremely rare Black Vulture has a short, wide tail and pale patches near tips of black wings. Usually silent; when threatened, it hisses.

Two-toned wings with spread finger-like primaries, tiny head.

Bare red skin on adult's head (black on young).

Osprey
Pandion haliaetus

L 22″ | **WS** 64″

This fishing hawk breeds in the north in increasing numbers, and has been reintroduced in the Twin Cities. The back and upper wings are dark brown like an adult Bald Eagle's; the head is mostly white, with a thick dark eye line, dark tail, white belly, and small, strongly hooked black bill. The bend in the wing is accentuated by a black patch. The stick nest is usually conspicuous atop a snag, telephone pole, or nest platform; eagle nests are usually below the top tier of branches rather than at the pinnacle. Excitable and noisy near the nest, giving high-pitched, wimpy chirps.

Note black patch at bend of wing, white forewing and belly.

Large body and small head distinctive.

Bald Eagle

Haliaeetus leucocephalus

L 33" | **WS** 80"

Our national emblem can be seen year-round throughout. Adult has blackish brown body and wings, white head and tail, and large, hooked yellow bill. It takes 4 to 6 years to attain adult plumage; before that, it's mostly brown with varying amounts of white, much splotchier than the Golden Eagle, which never has any whitish on the belly or back. The Bald Eagle often feeds on carrion near roadsides; also drawn to farm fields for poultry parts spread as fertilizer. Movies and TV commericals often show a Bald Eagle with a Red-tailed Hawk voice-over. Real Bald Eagles give loud, wimpy chirps.

Immature huge and splotchy; may have white on belly or back.

If head and tail disappear against bright sky, wings look like a long plank.

Sharp-shinned Hawk

Accipiter striatus

L 11.5″ | **WS** 19″

Three accipiters, with short, rounded wings, a long tail, and
flap-flap-glide flight, are found here. The Sharp-shinned,
the tiniest, is abundant at Hawk Ridge from late August to
mid-October. During migration, it frequents backyards, but
virtually never nests in towns or urban parks, preferring
northern forests. It's rarely seen in winter, mostly in the south,
often at feeders. Almost exactly like Cooper's Hawk, adult
has slate-gray back and narrow, horizontal reddish barring
on breast and belly; immature is brown with dark vertical
streaks on the breast and belly. Sharp-shinned usually has a
more squared-off tail tip, sometimes notched in the center, and
the wings often jut forward in flight, giving it a small-headed
appearance. When perched, the cap blends with the nape. Gives
a frenetic *kek-kek-kek-kek* call.

Adult has rusty
horizontal barring
on breast and belly;
eye may be yellow,
orange, or red.

Immature has vertical streaks on breast and belly; eye is yellow.

Wings curve a bit forward, neck doesn't appear thick, long tail fairly squared off.

Cooper's Hawk

Accipiter cooperii

L 15 " | **WS** 30"

This accipiter grabs birds at feeders year-round and nests in towns, cities, and urban parks, mostly in the south and central areas. Almost identical to smaller Sharp-shinned; in both, female much larger than males. Wings of Cooper's are usually held straight when gliding, the thick-necked head extending beyond wings. Closed tail has a rounded tip, and the neck and nape are paler than the black crown on the flattened head. Very common in the Twin Cities, but the least common accipiter at Hawk Ridge. Quiet except in the nesting season. Both sexes defend the nest with loud, grating *kak-kak-kak* calls.

Adult's black cap contrasts with pale nape. Round tail tip.

"Bull-necked" appearance and rounded tail.

Northern Goshawk

Accipiter gentilis

L 21-25 " | **WS** 40-46"

This bulky accipiter, a species of Special Concern, breeds in the forested north, hunting grouse, snowshoe hares, and other large prey. Irruptive migrant, most often and easily seen in October and November at Hawk Ridge, the only hawk-watching site in the Lower 48 where goshawks outnumber Cooper's Hawks; even there, though, sightings are usually few and far between. Adult steel-gray with fine horizontal barring on underparts; never has reddish breast and belly. Young bulkier than other accipiters. Broad-winged Hawks flying between woodlots may be mistaken for this much rarer species.

Adult with black cap and eye line, fine barring on breast.

Immature bulkier than other accipiters.

Northern Harrier

Circus hudsonius

L 19" | **WS** 43"

This slim, buoyant "marsh hawk," found in open pastures and marshes throughout, may overwinter in large fields. The face is owl-like, and it shares its habitat and hunting methods with the Short-eared Owl. Side-to-side teetering flight is accentuated by the long, slender wings and tail and white rump. Adult male steel-gray above and white below, with black wingtips, like a gull. Female and immature male brown. One male may mate with several females. During the breeding season, often gives a rapid series of high *kek-kek-kek* notes. Like some owls, the smaller male has a deeper voice than the larger female.

The most owl-like of hawks.

Adult male is nicknamed "gray ghost."

Red-shouldered Hawk

Buteo lineatus

L 20″ | **WS** 40″

This broad-winged, short-tailed hawk is designated Special Concern here. It breeds in moist forests in the southeastern half and occasionally winters. Seldom sits in the open as Red-taileds do. Banded tail of adult shows more white bands than the single one of the Broad-winged, and the black bands are wider than the white. Tail bands on young subtle; breast dark. In flight, the adult's red "shoulders" are visible from above. The wing shows a translucent curved "window" near the dark tip; often seems to reach forward when the bird glides. Blue Jays often mimic the whining *kee-ah* call.

Adult has rusty barring on underparts, white spots on wings.

Translucent crescent "windows" near wingtips; subtly banded tail in immature.

Broad-winged Hawk

Buteo platypterus

L 15″ | **WS** 34″

Our smallest buteo breeds in forests throughout. Hunts for small prey in woods from a perch. Adult's rusty breast bars and immature's vertical streaking similar to accipiters; Broad-winged has dark eyes, a chunky body, and short tail. In flight between woods, can be mistaken for rare Goshawk. Migration concentrated; thousands may be tallied at Hawk Ridge on a single September day, when most of the birds in the "kettles" (swarms of hawks circling on rising air currents) will be this species. Adult shows whitish wings edged with black from the tip through the trailing edge, as if outlined in black crayon; the tail appears black with a wide white band. Juvenile is the same size and shape. Call a plaintive but piercing two-noted whistle, the first note quick: *kee-eeeeeeee.*

Fairly small, chunky buteo; hunts from branches or power poles in forest, not skittish.

Adult in flight has pale wings outlined on trailing edge with black. Dark tail has one wide white band.

Immature's tail bands inconspicuous, dark trailing edge of the wings subtle. A bit bigger than a crow.

Swainson's Hawk
Buteo swainsoni

L 19-22" | **WS** 47.2-54.3"

This large prairie buteo is a very rare migrant. It breeds in the west, and is never present in winter. Many Red-taileds are misidentified as this species. Extremely variable plumage; fairly solid dark back, and except in all-dark birds, the head and breast are darker than the belly. In flight, long wings taper to a point; the trailing edge is darker than the forewing except in all-dark birds. Long tail, with dark terminal band, is often spread wide. Feet surprisingly small; hunts small prey, including grasshoppers. The shrill *kreeeee* alarm call and a few softer sounds are given mainly during nesting.

Typical adult with dark back, head, and upper breast; whitish belly.

Trailing edge of wings usually darker than forewings.

Red-tailed Hawk

Buteo jamaicensis

L 20″ | **WS** 48.5″

This extremely variable buteo is the most widespread and common raptor from spring through fall, and winters locally. A large hawk on a pole or wire along highway is usually a Red-tailed. Only adult has red tail, often not visible from beneath. Note the dark line (the patagial bar) along the leading edge of the wing from the neck to the bend of the wing, the dark comma-shaped wrist mark, and the dark feathers across the belly forming a belly band, all usually visible except on darkest birds. The screaming *keeeeee-arr* is an iconic sound, often used as a voice-over for Bald Eagles on TV and in movies.

Dark patagial bar, wing comma, and belly band.

The red tail is conspicuous on adults from some angles. Often sit in the open while watching for prey.

Rough-legged Hawk

Buteo lagopus

L 18-20" | **WS** 52-54"

This large tundra-breeding species is a migrant and winter visitor in open country throughout, more common in some years than others. Well-feathered legs give it its name. Plumage is variable, but usually shows a solid black belly band and white at the base of the tail; the wings are outlined in black from the tips through the trailing edge, and there is a large black mark on the wrist. Those marks are more obscure on dark-plumaged birds, but white at the base of the tail evident. The bill is much smaller than a Golden Eagle's. Seldom heard south of the breeding grounds.

Black belly band and wrist marks, white base of the tail.

Black belly band more solid than Red-tailed's.

Golden Eagle

Aquila chrysaetos

L 30" | **WS** 80"

This huge, fierce hunter is a rare migrant throughout and an occasional winter visitor, mostly in the southeast. Adults are all-dark, with golden feathers on the nape and a large bill. Until they're about five, young birds have fairly clean whitish patches on the wings and tail; they never have whitish feathers on the belly or breast. The wings sometimes appear to "pinch in," tapering slightly where they meet the body, especially on young birds. Golden Eagles are much quieter than Bald Eagles, seldom calling outside the nesting season.

Adult has long, all-dark wings and an all-dark body and tail. Note the golden nape feathers.

Virginia Rail

Rallus limicola

L 9″ | **WS** 14″

Rails are secretive marsh birds with chicken-like posture, a deliberate walk, and a tiny triangular tail that is white beneath; they're much more often heard than seen. The fairly common Virginia nests in reedy marshes throughout the state. Its distinctive gray cheeks contrast with rusty neck and breast. Flanks and lower belly are barred black and white. The similar King Rail, designated Endangered and last seen in the state in 1992, is much larger. Calls include a variety of pig-like grunts and a distinctive *kidick-kidick-kidick*; it sometimes responds to a birder's poor imitation.

Longish downcurved bill, gray cheeks, rusty neck and breast.

Yellow Rail
Coturnicops noveboracensis

L 5-7″ | **WS** 11-13″

This extremely rare bird, a species of Special Concern, breeds locally in sedge marshes in the northwest and north central, most often reported in Aitkin County. It's tiny and secretive, chunky with subtle markings and a rather thick yellow or dark bill. Diagnostic white wing patches are even harder to see than the rest of the bird. The tail is almost nonexistent. With patience and luck, you may locate a calling Yellow Rail moving stealthily near the edge of a marsh, especially before dawn. The distinctive call sounds like two stones clacking: *tic-tic, tic-tic-tic; tic-tic, tic-tic-tic.*

Small, yellowish; wing patches mostly hidden on folded wing.

Sora

Porzana carolina

L 8.5″ | **WS** 14″

This fairly common rail is found spring to fall in marshes throughout. Secretive, but sometimes walks through open channels or along edge of dense vegetation. Black and white barring on flanks and lower belly, gray face, brown back with white streaks, and triangular tail are distinctive when you're lucky enough to see one. Fairly short yellow or greenish bill (dusky on immatures) and, on breeding adult, black face and throat patch easily distinguish it from our other rails. Gives a distinctive long, descending whinny; a rising, piercing *ker-wee*; a *keep-keep-keep* call; and a single *keep* note.

Breeding adult has black mask.

Common Gallinule

Gallinula galeata

L 13" | **WS** 23"

This rare marsh bird, designated Special Concern, breeds locally in the south. Thick-bodied and small-headed with a red forehead shield, short, thick bill, and tiny triangular tail with white beneath. Those features and its habit of pumping its head when swimming distinguish it from ducks. Very long, thin toes allow it to walk on lily pads. Horizontal white streak along side and red bill distinguish from coots; may show a purplish blue sheen that coot never does. Very vocal, making a variety of clucks, yelps, and cackles, some similar to the much more common and widespread coot.

Note red bill, white streak on side, and triangular tail.

American Coot

Fulica americana

L 16" | **WS** 24"

The common, sociable "cute coot with its white snoot" is entirely dark gray except for the white bill and seldom noticed triangular undertail. Swimming coot pumps its neck back and forth. A favorite prey of eagles; when an eagle approaches, an entire flock may burst into action, pattering noisily on the water's surface before getting airborne. Spends more time in the open, on water or land, than other rails or gallinules. The greenish toes have thick lobes, fun to notice when a coot is standing on shore. Gives a variety of grunts, cackles, and clucking calls, often lower-pitched than calls of gallinules.

In good light, look for the red eye.

No white on plumage except beneath tail.

Sandhill Crane

Antigone canadensis

L 47" | **WS** 78.5"

Found spring through fall throughout, in pairs, family groups, or flocks. Fresh plumage gray; smears mud on feathers, staining them brown if iron present. Forehead and crown skin bumpy and bald, brilliant red when flushed with excitement. Weighs twice as much as the similarly sized Great Blue Heron; unlike heron, flies with neck fully extended and wings flat on both up- and downstroke, the supple feather tips curling up and down with the wingbeats. Huge, white Whooping Crane extremely rare; any sighting requires documentation. Guttural, weirdly trilling trumpeting calls carry a long distance.

Head and neck straight, balancing long legs.

When molting, old iron-stained feathers stand out.

American Avocet

Recurvirostra americana

L 16.9-18.5" | **WS** 32.2"

This large prairie shorebird is a rare breeder in the west, where most spring to fall sightings are concentrated, especially at Salt Lake in Lac Qui Parle County; rare and unpredictable elsewhere. During nesting, head, neck, and breast are pinkish brown; they turn soft grayish white by fall. Legs are grayish blue. Year-round, the black wings have a large white patch from the shoulder to the center of the back; extremely rare Black-necked Stilt has straight bill, no white wing patch, and long pink legs. Usually quiet, but sometimes gives a *kweep* alarm call that sounds a little like a yellowlegs.

Upcurved bill. Breeding adult with pinkish brown head.

Fall birds a study in black and white.

Black-bellied Plover

Pluvialis squatarola

L 11" | **WS** 23"

Our largest plover, the Black-bellied appears on shores and short grass fields throughout, most reliably at Park Point in Duluth. In all plumages, easily confused with American Golden-Plover when the wings are closed. In breeding plumage, Black-bellied's white neck feathers extend to the crown, and black belly ends at the legs, with white in front of the tail. In fall, often more grayish than brown. In any plumage, when wings are spread, note the Black-bellied's white rump, white wing stripe, and black "wingpits." Gives high, clear, sad-sounding notes a bit like a pewee.

Spring adult with white crown, white undertail.

Fall birds grayish, with little contrast between cap and eyebrow.

American Golden-Plover

Pluvialis dominica

L 9–11″ | **WS** 22″

The American Golden-Plover, found during migration on shores and short grass fields throughout, most regularly at Park Point in Duluth, is a bit smaller than the Black-bellied, but this is noticeable only when the two are side by side. It often has a soft golden-brown cast, but this is subtle, and lighting can affect the appearance of both species. In spring, crown is black (white on Black-bellied), and underparts are entirely black to the tail. Never has a white rump, white stripe on wings, or black "wing-pits." Calls are piercing and urgent but rich: *quee-del.*

In spring, dark crown and black undertail.

Fall birds brownish; crown contrasts with eyebrow.

Semipalmated Plover

Charadrius semipalmatus

L 7″ | **WS** 14″

This common migrant on mudflats and muddy shorelines looks like a miniature Killdeer with a single breast band, but is chunkier, with a thicker neck. Unmarked back is as dark as wet sand; underparts snowy white. Breeding adult has bright yellow or orange legs and black-tipped orange bill. In fall, adult has duller legs and more subtly two-toned bill; immature has grayish legs and black bill. In all plumages, breast band is solid, narrower in center. The extremely rare Wilson's Plover is larger, with a proportionally much longer bill. In flight, gives one or more husky whistles, *choo-wee, choo-wee*.

Adult has black-tipped bill, yellow legs, complete breast band.

Immature is like adult, but black bill and grayish legs.

Piping Plover
Charadrius melodus

L 6.6–7" | **WS** 15.3"

This tiny endangered plover formerly nested on sandy beaches along Lake Superior and Lake of the Woods. Vulnerable to beachgoers and dogs, it's now rarely found on Lake of the Woods; appearances anywhere else during migration make the rare bird alert. Sturdy black-tipped bill and orange legs similar to Semipalmated's, but Piping's back, the color of dry sand, is much paler, and the breast band usually appears broken in the center. The extremely rare Snowy Plover is very similar but with a more slender, all-dark bill and gray or black legs. Named for clear, mellow whistles, *peep* or *peep-lo*.

Adult with black-tipped bill, orange legs, broken breast band.

Immature with sturdy dark bill, orange legs, broken breast band.

Killdeer

Charadrius vociferus

L 9″ | **WS** 18.5″

Our most common and widespread plover, found from spring to fall throughout. Nests away from water on bare patches in fields and meadows, and even driveways and flat roofs. Solid brown above with a rusty tail and pure white underparts with two black breast bands. Face markings, white collar, and brilliant red eye rings are distinctive. More slender than smaller plovers. In flight or when giving a "broken wing display," the rusty tail is a great field mark. Extremely vocal, its *kill-deeah* pierces the air even in urban habitats as it flies over; it's often heard at night.

The double breast band is unique.

Rusty tail visible when wings are open.

Spotted Sandpiper

Actitis macularius

L 7.5″ | **WS** 15″

This fairly common bird of lakeshores, often seen on rocks and piers, bobs its tail persistently. Spring and summer adult has brown back (any flecking is dark rather than white), heavy spotting on white underparts, slightly downcurved orange bill, and pale legs. Non-breeding adult and young are plain-backed with pure white underparts; a small white area before the folded wing accentuates a large dusky smudge below the neck. Rapid, shallow wing beats, with wings held in a stiff arc; note white wing stripe and dark rump and tail. Often gives string of sharp *weet, weet-weet, weet-weet* notes.

Breeding adult has spotted breast, dark back, long orange bill.

Fall birds are unspotted. Note brownish smudge on the side.

Solitary Sandpiper

Tringa solitaria

L 7-9" | **WS** 16"

This common migrant is usually solitary, but may be found in small groups; rarely seen in summer in northern Cook County. It nests in trees in boreal bogs, using abandoned nests of larger songbirds. Resembles yellowlegs, but legs are shorter and duller, eye ring more conspicuous, and rump dark. Whitish flecking on the back, fine, dark streaking across breast, and delicate, straight bill distinguish from the chunkier Spotted. In flight, the wings, rump, and center of the tail are dark; the outer tail feathers are mostly white with crossbars. It walks with a high-stepping gait and bobs its head. The shrill *peet-weet* calls are higher-pitched than the calls of the Spotted Sandpiper.

Dark breast, white flecking on dark back, white eye ring. In flight, rump and center of tail dark; outer tail has dark crossbars.

Greater Yellowlegs

Tringa melanoleuca

L 13.5″ | **WS** 27.5″

Both yellowlegs resemble Solitary Sandpiper except for their white rump, mostly white tail, more subtle eye ring, and long, yellow legs. Identifying which is which is more challenging, and there's no shame in letting one go as "unidentified yellow-legs species." Greater, much larger than Lesser, has a slightly thicker, often two-toned bill that is usually longer than head and often curves subtly upward. Greater is often very active while feeding. Both yellowlegs nicknamed "tattlers" because they call at the least disturbance. The Greater gives its *chu chu chu* or *tew tew tew* alarm calls in series of three or more.

Very long, slightly two-toned bill sweeps upward.

White rump and delicately barred tail, long yellow legs.

Lesser Yellowlegs

Tringa flavipes

L 10″ | **WS** 27″

Both yellowlegs are common migrants throughout. The Lesser's bill is entirely black and straight, and roughly the same length as the head. It feeds in more leisurely fashion than the Greater Yellowlegs, picking delicately at prey. Compared to the Solitary Sandpiper, the legs are brighter and longer, and any eye ring is less conspicuous. It often gathers in flocks with other shorebirds, including Greaters. The calls of this "tattletale" are similar to those of Greater, but usually given as well-spaced single or double notes rather than in threes or more: *tew, tew-tew, tew.*

Bright yellow legs and straight, delicate black bill.

Like Greater but with more delicate, all-black bill.

Willet

Tringa semipalmata

L 12.9–16″ | **WS** 27.5″

This uncommon or rare spring migrant, a bit larger than the Greater Yellowlegs, was once a regular summer resident in the south and west. It can seem nondescript at first view, with softly grayish, dull plumage and dull gray legs, but it undergoes an amazing transformation when it opens its wings to reveal the bold, eye-catching black and white wing pattern. The most distinctive call, a sharp *pill-will-willet*, is given mostly in breeding season. Other calls, many rather raucous, are given year-round.

Nondescript, with sturdy bluish-gray legs and heavy bill.

Dramatic black and white wing pattern.

Upland Sandpiper

Bartramia longicauda

L 11-12" | **WS** 18-22"

This lithe sandpiper of meadows and prairies, most common in the west, is usually found far from water, often perched on rocks, hay bales, or fence posts with a distinctive erect stance. The large dark eyes on a fairly plain face and the long, slender neck are distinctive. It arrives to breed, mostly in the west, in late April and May; most are gone by early August. The most distinctive call is the flight display's "wolf whistle," a long rising note followed by a mournful, descending note; it is often heard above displaying prairie-chickens. It also gives rolling, purring call notes.

Medium-length yellowish legs, lithe neck, and large dark eyes; often sits on a conspicuous perch.

Whimbrel

Numenius phaeopus

L 17.3″ | **WS** 32″

In May and early June, birders check out the rocky shoreline along the North Shore and the grassy fields and shoreline at Park Point in Duluth searching for this rare and local but regular migrant, which is seldom seen at other places or times. Speckled brownish overall with paler underparts; dark eye line and crown stripe contrast with pale eyebrow. The only other shorebird with a very long downcurved bill, the much rarer Long-billed Curlew, is more buffy or light cinnamon; sightings would require documentation. Whimbrels are seldom heard here, but may give a rapid series of hollow whistles.

Bold eye line and crown stripe, long downcurved bill.

Hudsonian Godwit

Limosa haemastica

L 14–17" | **WS** 27"

The two godwits in our state both have long, slightly upturned, bicolored bills. The Hudsonian appears here only during migration, mostly in the west. Any chestnut coloring is mostly restricted to the breast and underparts, but in spring it can occasionally be mistaken for a Marbled Godwit. Non-breeding Hudsonian is usually grayer than Marbled. If you're not certain, wait for it to fly to see the Hudsonian's black tail with a white base and fairly conspicuous wing stripe. Usually quiet, but occasionally gives a high-pitched, rising *pid-wit* call.

Breeding bird has at least some chestnut on underparts.

Non-breeding bird is fairly gray.

Marbled Godwit

Limosa fedoa

L 16.5–18.8" | **WS** 31"

This godwit, designated a species of Special Concern, breeds very locally in prairies, meadows, and pastures in the northwest and west-central part of the state. Marbleds in all plumages are soft tawny brown overall with an extremely long, black-tipped pinkish bill. In flight, the tail is brown with no white base, and the wings are orangey cinnamon and black with no white wing stripe. Few sightings after mid-August. The flight call, heard especially in breeding areas, is a nasal, hoarse *kah-wek*, lower than the Hudsonian's.

Tawny shorebird of the prairie; no white on wings or tail.

Similar to Hudsonian Godwit; soft tawny overall.

Ruddy Turnstone

Arenaria interpres

L 7" | **WS** 21"

This squat, stocky shorebird is an uncommon migrant on beaches and rocky shores of larger lakes; most often seen on Lake Superior, usually in small flocks. Ruddy only in breeding plumage, it is strikingly patterned rufous, black, and white. More dully colored non-breeding birds show a hint of the spring pattern. Note bright orange legs and short, thick black bill; the angle of the lower mandible is adapted for turning stones to reveal food. White back, wing stripes, and tail conspicuous in flight. It gives rapid twittering and chuckling sounds.

Breeding birds with short bill, clownish face, and bold markings.

Non-breeding birds show same overall pattern, bright legs, short bill.

Red Knot

Calidris canutus

L 9-10" | **WS** 20.5-22.0"

This rare migrant, federally designated as Threatened, is sometimes spotted at Park Point in Duluth in late May or from late
August into early September. Related to the tiniest sandpipers,
the "peeps," but much larger. Red breeding plumage, plump
body, short legs, and dappled back are superficially like a
dowitcher; the Knot has a short bill and paler crown. Nondescript in non-breeding plumage: soft, fairly solid gray above
and pale below. Immature has delicate flecks on the throat,
breast, and flanks. All ages have a soft gray rump and tail.
Seldom heard in Minnesota, but gives a soft *ka-whit* in flight.

Breeding adult rich
rust on face and
breast, fairly short bill.

Immature with pale
edging on back feathers;
short, straight bill.

Stilt Sandpiper

Calidris himantopus

L 8.5" | **WS** 16.5"

This medium-sized sandpiper, a common migrant throughout, especially in fall, has longer neck and legs than peeps. Breeding adult has chestnut ear patch, heavily barred belly, and splotchy back. When wings are folded, the patterned back is darker than the unpatterned wings. Immature and non-breeding adult more nondescript. The fairly long bill droops at the tip like a Dunlin's. In flight, all-white rump and pale gray tail; no wing stripes. Associates with dowitchers; the Stilt has longer legs and a much shorter bill. The call is rather frog-like, a rising, trilling *querp*.

Breeding adult shows heavy barring beneath and a rusty ear patch.

Non-breeding nondescript, with fairly long neck and legs, drooped bill.

Sanderling
Calidris alba

L 7.5″ | **WS** 13.5″

This active little sandpiper, described by Roger Tory Peterson as moving like a clockwork toy, is an uncommon migrant along lakeshores, especially Lake Superior. Breeding male has dark rufous head and neck; all other plumages have snow-white underparts. Overall paler than other sandpipers. Sturdy black bill droops; black legs and feet with no hind toe. Underwing white; upper surface of wing is black, with a bold white wing stripe. Flocks run along beaches as if in panic mode: "Oh, no! There goes the water! Oh, no! Here comes the water!" Often gives conversational twitterings and *kip* notes.

Non-breeding birds with white underparts, from lower face to tail.

Breeding male has rusty color more restricted than in Red Knot.

Dunlin

Calidris alpina

L 7" | **WS** 14.5"

This squat, pudgy migrant, fairly common in spring and fall throughout but especially in Duluth, has short legs and a fairly long, tapering bill that droops at the tip. Its old name, Red-backed Sandpiper, fits breeding adult, which also has a large rectangular black belly patch. Juvenile reddish with a hint of black flecking on the belly; non-breeding adult grayer with white underparts. Often found in groups; one or two Dunlin in breeding plumage can help identify the others. Gives a few harsh, raspy calls, some transcribed as *kree kree kree*.

The large rectangular belly patch is unique.

Seems hunched and dumpy; long, tapering bill droops.

Least Sandpiper
Calidris minutilla

L 6.5″ | **WS** 16.5″

"Peeps" are tiny sandpipers in the genus *Calidris*, often seen in mixed flocks. Leg color and where the wingtips end relative to the tail are important to note. The Least, an abundant migrant, is our smallest shorebird. It's easy to tell from other peeps if you can see the yellow legs. Unfortunately, that can be hard in poor light or if the legs are coated with mud. When peeps feed together, this is the smallest and darkest, and often the one farthest from water. The slender bill has a slight droop; that of the Semipalmated is usually straight. Gives a high, plaintive *kree*.

Yellow legs; bill has a slight droop.

Diagnostic yellowish legs can be hard to see.

Semipalmated Sandpiper

Calidris pusilla

L 5.5" | **WS** 11"

This common peep usually has a straight bill, but it may occasionally droop a bit, leading to confusion with the extremely rare Western Sandpiper. In a large mixed flock, a few Semipalmateds may stand out with a slightly droopy bill, but if you're looking at a tiny peep and the wingtips don't extend past the tail, and if it has black legs, assume it's this one. The Least has yellow legs, and is usually slightly darker and more distinctly marked on the breast. The call is a short *churk*.

Black legs, short wing, and straight bill.

Bill may appear to have a slight droop.

Baird's Sandpiper
Calidris bairdii

L 6-7" | **WS** 14-15"

Baird's, an uncommon migrant, is associated with grassy
habitats. It's one of the "peeps," tiny sandpipers in the genus
Calidris. On perched birds, it is important to note where the
wingtips end relative to the tail. Baird's and White-rumped are
the two peeps with wingtips extending slightly beyond the tail.
Baird's has a soft buffy breast, and is lighter and more evenly
toned than the White-rumped. Baird's always has a dark rump,
visible when the wings are open. Gives a low-pitched rolling
call, higher and more mellow than Pectoral's.

Wingtips project
beyond tail;
plumage rather
buffy.

White-rumped Sandpiper
Calidris fuscicollis

L 6.5" | **WS** 16.5"

This migrant is uncommon in spring, rarer in fall, mostly near
Lake Superior. Less buffy than Baird's. Our only peep with a
white rump. Gives a *jeet* call, much higher-pitched than Baird's;
sometimes twitters like an Eastern Kingbird.

Wingtips project
beyond tail;
darker and less
buffy than Baird's.

Pectoral Sandpiper

Calidris melanotos

L 8.5" | **WS** 17"

A size up from the closely related peeps, this common migrant throughout has greenish or yellowish legs and a slightly drooping bill like the Least Sandpiper, but is much larger. The breast is heavily streaked, the dark color ending abruptly with a clean demarcation from the white belly. When it takes off, it often flies in a zigzag pattern; the wings are all-dark. The call is a low, rich *churk*.

Bigger than a Least, our only peep with yellow legs.

Dense breast streaking ends cleanly at the white belly.

Short-billed Dowitcher

Limnodromus griseus

L 11″ | **WS** 19″

The two dowitchers, both with long bills, probe into mud straight up and down in a sewing-machine action. Snipe-like in shape, but lacking the snipe's striped crown and back. Knot-like in color, but with a much longer bill and darker crown. Telling the two dowitcher species apart except by calls is hard even for experts. One seen here from mid-May to early September is likely to be Short-billed, which is also slightly more common. Short-billed is quiet while feeding, and in flight it gives a mellow *tu tu tu* that often descends in pitch, lower-pitched than Long-billed's call.

Breeding bird has Red Knot's color but darker crown, very long bill.

Always easier to tell from Long-billed by voice.

Long-billed Dowitcher

Limnodromus scolopaceus

L 11.4" | **WS** 18.1"

If you see a dowitcher here before late April or after mid-September, it's much more likely to be this one, though overall it's slightly less common than the Short-billed. In breeding plumage, it's darker above and more heavily spotted or barred beneath; the tail usually has wider black than white bars. Young bird may be brighter above and a bit rustier below. The most reliable way to tell this species from the Short-billed is by voice. Feeding Long-billeds constantly chatter with soft, high notes; in flight, they give a high, sharp *keet, keet*, sometimes accelerating into a quick *kik-kik-kik-kik*.

In spring, bold white tips on dark shoulder feathers.

Dowitchers chattering while feeding are Long-billeds.

Buff-breasted Sandpiper
Calidris subruficollis

L 7–7.8″ | **WS** 16.5″

This rare fall migrant, seen almost exclusively from late July through September, has soft brown plumage and large eyes; it looks a bit like a miniature Upland Sandpiper or a cross between a sandpiper and a dove. The delicate bill is rather short and straight. It's often found in short grass, especially at sod farms throughout the state, and occasionally visits sand beaches, especially along the North Shore and at Park Point in Duluth. It's virtually never seen here in spring. It gives a series of soft clicking notes and a soft *churr*.

Dove-like with round head, large eyes, short slender bill, and soft brown plumage.

Wilson's Snipe

Gallinago delicata

L 11.5″ | **WS** 17″

Often hidden in plain sight along edges of ponds or in muddy fields, the snipe occasionally sits conspicuously on fence posts or power poles. It breeds throughout, and may rarely be seen in winter near open water. It's easy to recognize by the bold stripes on the back and head. In flight, the short wings are more narrow and pointed than a woodcock's. Gives loud *chick, chick, chick* calls. The "winnowing" flight display sound, produced by specialized tail feathers, is a haunting crescendo: *hu-hu-hu-hu-hu-hu-hu-HOO!* heard over grasslands and marshes.

Our only long-billed shorebird that sits on fence posts; white stripes on head and back not always visible.

American Woodcock

Scolopax minor

L 11″ | **WS** 18″

This plump, short-legged shorebird with an extremely long bill and buffy orange underparts breeds throughout most of the state. Unlike snipe, the striping on a woodcock's head runs across the crown, and the wider back striping is soft gray rather than white. Most are seen in clearings near wet woods while displaying at dusk in spring and early summer. When flushed, woodcock wings make the same twittering sound they do in flight displays. The *beep* call is softer and shorter than a night-hawk's *peent*. One may give this call dozens of times before taking off in the flight display.

Note gray stripes on the back, transverse stripes on the head, and orange underparts.

Wilson's Phalarope

Phalaropus tricolor

L 8.6-9.4" | **WS** 16.5"

Phalaropes are dainty shorebirds that use their lobed feet to swim, often spinning in circles to stir up food. Wilson's is the only one that breeds in Minnesota, mainly in grassy marshes in the western and central counties; uncommon and local, it's designated Threatened here. Its needle-like bill, improbably thin, is noticeably longer than the head. Female is more colorful than male. In non-breeding bird, note thin bill and white face without an ear patch. In flight, there is no wing stripe and the rump is white. Calls include a low, nasal bark and a quiet purr.

Breeding female gray, white, and peachy; maroon brown neck.

Non-breeding birds gray, with eye line and needle-like bill.

Red-necked Phalarope

Phalaropus lobatus

L 6-8" | **WS** 13"

This uncommon migrant is found mostly on large sewage ponds in the west in May. The bill is shorter than Wilson's (about the length of the head) and less astonishingly narrow. Always has a dark patch behind the eye, and shows a conspicuous white wing stripe in flight; the tail is dark, and the dark rump is bordered with white. The extremely rare Red Phalarope (most often seen on Lake Superior) has a thicker, paler bill; in breeding plumage, it's red beneath with a white cheek, but is noticeably paler in non-breeding plumage. Flight call is a sharp *ket* call sounding like a blackbird.

Bill as long as head; throat and central breast not rusty.

Dark mark behind the eye.

Parasitic Jaeger

Stercorarius parasiticus

L 21" | **WS** 21"

This rare visitor is most regularly seen in Duluth area in fall. All three jaegers have pale shafts to outer wing feathers, visible from a long distance. The most likely of the three is the Parasitic, which has a dark bill and two pointed central feathers sticking out beyond the tapered tail. Juvenile's tips may not stick out far, but are always pointed. Those tips are rounded in the thicker-bodied Pomarine Jaeger, which has a pale, dark-tipped bill. The tail tips are very long in the extremely rare Long-tailed Jaeger, which is smaller and daintier than the gulls it harasses.

White shafts on the primary wing feathers in all jaegers. Parasitic's spiky tail feathers are pointed; its bill is black.

Bonaparte's Gull

Chroicocephalus philadelphia

L 13" | **WS** 30.5"

Minnesota's most widespread black-headed gull in spring and
fall, this dainty bird may appear in small groups or large flocks
on lakes throughout the state. Breeding adult's entire head, not
just the crown, is black, with small white crescent above and
below the eye. Non-breeding adult and young have white head
with a dark spot behind ear. Adult's primary wing feathers
white edged with black; in flight, they form a distinctive white
wedge. In all plumages, Bonaparte's has pink or red legs and
a black bill. It occasionally gives buzzy, tern-like sounds like
bweh-bweh-bweh.

Breeding adult has
black bill, subtle eye
crescents, red legs.

Nonbreeding birds
have black bill, ear
spot, pink legs.

Franklin's Gull

Leucophaeus pipixcan

L 13-14" | **WS** 33-37"

This black-headed gull nests locally in the west. It can be abundant, but water levels and disturbances dramatically affect numbers from year to year, so the species is designated Special Concern. The nesting colony at Agassiz National Wildlife Refuge is one of the largest in the world. Often follows plows to feed on exposed worms, insects, and mice. Breeding adult has more conspicuous white eye crescents than Bonaparte's, a deep red bill, and black legs. Immature and non-breeding adult have dark "half hood" with white at base of dark bill. Calls are squeaky and nasal.

Breeding adult with eye crescents, deep red bill, black legs.

Non-breeding bird has mostly dark head, legs black.

Sabine's Gull

Xema sabini

L 13.5″ | **WS** 33″

Any gull with solid black outer wing feathers from above is a rare species. The dainty Sabine's Gull shows up in September or early October, especially on large lakes. Adult has dark head, white tail, and black bill with yellow tip. Immature has dark nape and back, black at end of tail, no yellow on bill. The even rarer Black-legged Kittiwake has a black collar and M pattern on wings. In its first winter, Ross's Gull, recorded in the state only three times, can have similar wing pattern with a black-tipped, wedge-shaped tail. Call is a grating, tern-like *kyeer kyeer*.

From above, primaries are solid black; from below, just the tips are black.

Tip of black bill is yellow. In flight look for notched tail.

Ring-billed Gull

Larus delawarensis

L 19" | **WS** 43.5"

This abundant gull mooches from picnickers, feeds on new-mown pastures, and acts like a normal "seagull." May remain in winter near open water, including Lake Superior. Adult has a black ring on the yellow bill, yellow legs and feet. Adult head white in spring and summer, lightly smudged in fall and winter. Immature is paler than young Herring, with a cleaner terminal tail band; may have pinkish legs and feet. Wings dark-tipped in all plumages. Side by side, much smaller than Herring; seems less burly. Gives a variety of mostly high-pitched calls; it takes practice to tell from Herring.

Adult shows yellow feet and "ring" around yellow bill.

Immature's dark terminal tail band contrasts with white tail.

Herring Gull

Larus argentatus

L 24" | **WS** 55.5"

This abundant gull is more barrel-chested, with a thicker bill,
than Ring-billed. When resting side by side, the Herring's larger
size is obvious. Adult Herring's bill is yellow with a red spot
near the tip; feet are pink or flesh-colored; in winter, head
more streaked. Immature is darker than young Ring-billed; the
wider terminal tail band contrasts less with the rest of the tail.
Birders gather at Canal Park in Duluth on winter days to study
gulls, often at close range, when less common visitors join the
Herrings. Thayer's and Iceland are very similar to Herring; both
average a bit smaller than Herring (seldom noticeably so), with
a smaller, rounder head, more delicate bill, and (usually) paler
plumage. Herring gives a variety of calls, many lower in pitch
than Ring-billed.

Breeding adult has sturdy
yellow bill with red spot near
lower tip, pinkish legs and
feet, head all white.

Young bird is darker, larger, and more robust than Ring-billed. Blackish tip on pinkish bill.

Very dark in first winter. The wide terminal tail band is distinct but much less contrasting than Ring-billed's.

Glaucous Gull

Larus hyperboreus

L 26″ | **WS** 58.6–71.6″

Larger than Herring Gull, with pure white wingtips, this uncommon but regular winter visitor is fairly easy to pick out in a large flock of gulls, most often on Lake Superior or in the Twin Cities from November through March. Iceland Gull and other outlier gulls with white wingtips would be at least slightly smaller than Herring Gull and much smaller than Glaucous. Bill on immatures pinkish with black tip, on adults yellowish with red mark near tip. Calls similar to those of Herring Gull.

Huge size, bulky body and bill, white wing tips.

Adult is white with solid gray back and wings, white wingtips.

Great Black-backed Gull

Larus marinus

L 30″ | **WS** 65″

This enormous gull, the "king of the Atlantic waterfront," is a
rare migrant and winter visitor on Lake Superior; sightings
have been increasing in recent years. One or two may be found
in mixed gull flocks dominated by Herring Gulls; often seen
at Canal Park in Duluth with other gulls in winter. At all ages,
it's huge, dwarfing even Glaucous Gulls. Adult unmistakable.
Young bird's underparts are paler and less splotchy than on
young Herring Gull, but the back is conspicuously darker. Calls
are much lower and hoarser than those of Herring Gull.

Adult with yellow bill, pink legs
and feet, white wingtips.
Immature has darker back,
paler underparts than Herring.

Caspian Tern

Hydroprogne caspia

L 20″ | **WS** 50″

Our largest, bulkiest tern looks almost like a gull. It migrates throughout, and breeds very locally in the north-central part of the state. It shares a black cap and colorful bill with Common and Forster's Tern, but is much more robust, both perched and in flight, and doesn't have such a deeply forked tail. Unlike our small gulls, the entire crown is black, but the throat is white. For such graceful birds, terns give surprisingly raspy, grating calls. This one sounds a bit like a heron, throatier than the smaller terns.

Robust orange bill, short black legs, black cap.

Tail shorter than other terns, body beefier.

Black Tern

Chlidonias niger

L 9.5" | **WS** 23"

This elegant tern breeds in grassy marshes throughout except
in the far northeast. Mostly present between May and August,
but has declined dramatically in recent decades. It's usually
seen in buoyant, swallow-like flight, close to the water, its
black head and breast sandwiched between silvery gray wings.
The thin, straight bill is black. Young birds and non-breeding
adults are white beneath, with a dark crown and nape forming
"ear flaps." The calls are squeakier but just as cranky as those
of our white terns.

Breeding birds with black
head and breast, long wings,
thin dark bill.

Non-breeding plumage
mostly white; black cap forms
"ear flaps."

Common Tern

Sterna hirundo

L 12–15" | **WS** 30.5"

The "sea swallow" breeds locally in colonies on our largest
lakes; rare and declining, it's designated Threatened. Slightly
slimmer than Forster's Tern, with dark edge to tail and soft
grayish underparts in breeding plumage. In non-breeding
plumage has a white forehead and dark hind crown. In flight,
look for gray primary wing feathers with a dark wedge near
the wingtip. Very similar to the extremely rare Arctic Tern,
which has shorter legs: if one joins a line of Common Terns, it
will be noticeably shorter than the others. Call, very similar to
Forster's, is a raspy, descending *keeeer*.

Breeding birds with
black-tipped red bill,
soft grayish underparts.

Non-breeding and
juvenile have dark bill,
blackish hind-crown.

Forster's Tern
Sterna forsteri

L 13.5″ | **WS** 31″

This species of Special Concern breeds near lakes of the west, central, and south-central areas, and migrates throughout. In most areas, especially shallow lakes, ponds, and marshes, it's much more common in Minnesota than the Common Tern. Thin white edge on long forked tail; breeding adult has pure white underparts. In flight, silvery white primary wing feathers edged with just a bit of black. In non-breeding plumage, has a white crown, often flecked delicately with dark, and a black mask behind the eye. Sounds like Common Tern, but calls a bit lower pitched and even raspier.

Breeding birds with black-tipped orange bill; underparts pure white.

Non-breeding birds have whitish crown, black behind eye.

Rock Pigeon

Columba livia

L 13″ | **WS** 23″

Our familiar pigeon has been domesticated in Eurasia for millennia. Plumage varies from all white to all dark, gray to reddish, often marked with white or black. Has a white fleshy bulge called a cere at the base of the bill; the rump is usually white. The wings are sharply pointed; in flight, can be mistaken for a falcon. After taking off and reaching altitude, often holds the wings in a distinctive deep V, rocking back and forth for several seconds before flapping again. The voice is a deep, muffled, tremulous *cooooo*. The powerful wingbeats produce a clapping sound, especially on takeoff.

Most flocks include birds of different colors.

Reddish legs and white "cere" at the base of the bill.

Eurasian Collared-Dove

Streptopelia decaocto

L 11.5-11.75" | **WS** 18.5-21.6"

This feral pigeon, larger and paler than a Mourning Dove, with a blunter tail, is a recent arrival in Minnesota, now established as a permanent resident in the south and west and spreading to other areas. It has a darker, more delicate bill than a Rock Pigeon, and lacks the bulging white cere. In flight, it has white outer tail feathers; lacks the white rump and wing linings of paler Rock Pigeons. The call is a three-noted *coo-COOO-coop*, less breathy than a Mourning Dove's.

Soft brown head and breast, black collar. White outer tail feathers a bit like Mourning Dove's in flight, but tail blunt.

Mourning Dove
Zenaida macroura

L 11" | **WS** 17.5"

This backyard feeder bird is a common spring and summer resident throughout except in forested habitat; less common in winter, especially in north. Adult is brown with black spots on the wings and pinkish iridescence on neck, long pointed tail, and blue ring around the eye. Tail feathers have a black mark below the large white spot at the tip, revealed when tail is opened. Fairly independent juvenile may be noticeably smaller than adult; its feathers are more scaly. Call is a mellow, breathy *Hoo-HOOOOOah, hooo-hooo*. The wings make a soft, airy whistle on takeoff and sometimes while in flight.

Mostly soft brown with black wing spots, pinkish iridescence on neck, white along edge of pointed tail, and red feet.

Yellow-billed Cuckoo

Coccyzus americanus

L 11" | **WS** 16"

This long, lanky skulker breeds in the south and central areas, especially near tent caterpillar webs. Like similar Black-billed Cuckoo, it is brown with pure white underparts and an improbably long tail; Yellow-billed has much larger white spots under tail and the slightly curved bill mostly yellow. Rufous outer wing feathers, brown in Black-billed, mostly seen in flight. Wing lining is as white as belly. The "rain crow" often calls before and during rainfall, a guttural *tick-tick-tick-tick-COWP, COWP, COWP* call, and a series of identical mellow *croo, croo, croo, croo* notes, each descending in pitch.

Rufous wing feathers mostly hidden on closed wing.

White tail spots much larger than on Black-billed.

Black-billed Cuckoo

Coccyzus erythropthalmus

L 12″ | **WS** 16″

This cuckoo breeds throughout the state and is the only species in the northeast, where it can be abundant in years when forest tent caterpillars ("army worms") abound. Compared to the slightly larger Yellow-billed, its tail spots are smaller, and it lacks rufous in wing feathers. In flight, the wing linings are off-white, not pure white. Adult has red ring around eye; yellow in Yellow-billed. Two different calls are usually transcribed as *coo-coo-coo*. One is a clucking set of 2 to 4 rapid coo's, repeated over and over. The other is softer and more deliberate, sounding breathier.

All-black bill, small tail spots, no rufous in wings.

Eastern Screech-Owl

Megascops asio

L 8.5" | **WS** 20"

Our only tiny "eared" owl is a permanent resident except in the
north-central and northeast. It's compact and sturdy; the head
never looks rounded like the tinier Saw-whet Owl. The etched
plumage is usually gray, rarely rufous. Strictly nocturnal, it
roosts by day in cavities or Wood Duck boxes, occasionally
sticking its head out for a bit of sun. If one must roost out on
a branch, it hunkers down near the trunk to avoid detection.
Harassment by chickadees or other birds can help us notice
an owl. Calls include a long quiet trill on one note and a long
descending whinny. It seldom if ever screeches.

Tiny and tufted; protects eyes
from sunlight and from detection
by keeping eyelids mostly closed.

Great Horned Owl

Bubo virginianus

L 21.5" | **WS** 48.5"

Our most widespread owl, shaped like a plump tailless cat, has yellow eyes, feathered "horns," and a broad orange face. Found throughout except dense forests, it serves as a nocturnal counterpart to the Red-tailed Hawk, even nesting in old Red-tailed nests. Mobbing crows alert us to one roosting by day. Usually non-migratory, but Great Horned Owls from north, almost as white as Snowies, may appear in fall and winter. Hoots are soft and mellow: *hoo hoo HOOO, hoo hoo*. Male has a deeper voice, noticeable when a pair duets. Snaps bill when irritated. Young make various squeaky screeches.

Our only huge owl with feathered tufts; mostly rich brown. The white throat bulges when it's hooting.

Snowy Owl

Bubo scandiacus

L 20-28" | **WS** 50-57"

Our heaviest owl appears in the Duluth harbor, and here and there, every winter. In "invasion" years, it may show up just about anywhere, mostly on shorelines and fields that superficially resemble its tundra home. Its rounded head and yellow eyes in a white face are unlike any other owl; body plumage ranges from almost pure white to heavily spotted. Only rarely perches in trees; roosts by day on snow piles, power poles, and other solid structures. Usually sits tight but flies if disturbed by ravens, hawks, or people. It's seldom heard here, but when disturbed, may hiss and snap its bill.

White face distinctive, even with dark cap and plumage.

Whiter plumage typical of older birds.

Northern Hawk Owl

Surnia ulula

L 14-18" | **WS** 28"

Our most diurnal owl, a winter visitor and rare breeder in northern bogs, looks like a cross between an owl and a kestrel with its vertical black facial markings, habit of bobbing its tail when alighting, and use of the same conspicuous perches that kestrels use in summer. It superficially resembles the tiny Boreal Owl, but is proportionally much longer. It often flies in to inspect people and other large mammals, perhaps hoping to steal food as Canada Jays do. Seldom calls in winter; gives breeding call mostly at night: a trill more robust than that of screech-owl and faster than Boreal.

Yellow eyes and long tail; head appears squarish because of vertical facial marks. Sits on exposed perches.

Barred Owl

Strix varia

L 20″ | **WS** 42″

This common owl, found year-round in wet woods and forests, is absent only in the southwest. No other owl here except the extremely rare Barn Owl has brown eyes. That, the round head, and brown rather than orange cheeks distinguish it from the larger Great Horned Owl. The much larger Great Gray Owl has a relatively huge head, white "bow tie," and yellow eyes. Known for its loud, strident *Who cooks for you? Who cooks for you-all?* call, sometimes heard in daytime. At night, call escalates into a *whuh-whuh-whuh-WHOO-AHH* followed by bizarre, monkey-like calls. Begging young have a loud rising squeal.

No other owl has brown eyes, round head, and dark horizontal barring on the upper breast. Bill is bright yellow.

Great Gray Owl

Strix nebulosa

L 24–33" | **WS** 54–60"

This permanent resident of northern bogs is most often seen in the Sax-Zim Bog and similar habitat in Aitkin County. Rare or uncommon most years, it may appear in large or even huge numbers in winter during irruption years. The distinctive white "bow tie" can be seen in poor light from a surprising distance. Our longest owl, it weighs much less than Great Horned or Snowy, and often perches on surprisingly flimsy branches. It specializes on voles, usually eating little else. Call is a deep, resonant, steady *hoo, hoo, hoo, hoo, hoo*. Squawky alarm call is given near the nest.

Oversized head, fairly small, yellow eyes, and white "bow tie." Its body is surprisingly scrawny under the feathers.

Long-eared Owl

Asio otus

L 14.5" | **WS** 35–39"

This medium-sized owl breeds throughout except in the southwest. Over 100 migrants are banded every October at Hawk Ridge, and some overwinter. Much smaller and proportionally thinner than Great Horned, except when puffed out in alarm; feather tufts emerge much closer together than Great Horned's. Black "comma" at the bend of under wing and thick black mark at the bend of the upper wing similar to Short-eared; they may hunt over same fields. Crows often mob Long-eareds at roost in dense conifers. Breeding male's soft barking *hoot* given about once every 2 or 3 seconds. Females give a nasal, squeaky *beee-oh*.

Feather tufts close together; facial disks round.

Look for the black comma on underwing and the soft buffy color. The wing tips have narrow, delicate barring, and the body is dark from head through belly.

Short-eared Owl

Asio flammeus

L 15″ | **WS** 37″

This medium-sized owl, designated Special Concern, is a rare migrant and winter visitor throughout and breeds in the north-west. Nocturnal counterpart of the Northern Harrier, it's found in the same grassy and marshy areas, dunes, and similar open habitat; buoyant harrier-like flight. Active by day, especially in late afternoon. Similar in flight to Long-eared, but Short-eared has thicker dark band at wingtip, and belly is paler than head. Short-eared roosts in hidden spots, usually on the ground. Usually silent. Can give wheezy notes and nasal barks; breeding male gives a rapid, twangy *poo poo poo*.

The tiny "ear" feathers are usually not visible.

Black "comma" like Long-eared, but belly paler than head.

Boreal Owl

Aegolius funereus

L 8-10" | **WS** 22-23"

This tiny species of Special Concern draws birders to the
Duluth–Two Harbors area during "invasion" years. Screech-
owl-sized, but no "ears." A bit larger than Saw-whet; Boreal's
crown is spotted, not streaked, and back more evenly spotted.
Usually roosts in a cavity but sometimes in a conifer. Rarely
hunts in daytime. Finding one in winter can be a matter of
looking at the right branch at the right moment or of tracking
down scolding chickadees. On calm April nights, male gives a
loud *hoo hoo hoo hoo hoo HOO!* The rhythm is like a snipe's
winnowing, but the notes are more piercing.

Spotted forehead,
dark border to
facial disks, and
evenly spotted
back distinguish
from Saw-Whet.

Northern Saw-whet Owl

Aegolius acadicus

L 7.5″ | **WS** 17.5″

Our tiniest owl breeds in cavities in mixed aspen groves in the north and east, migrates throughout, and overwinters here and there. Fall movement peaks on September and October nights, when about 1,000 are banded at Hawk Ridge and many at other banding stations. Soft facial markings give it an innocent look. Roosts quietly by day, usually near a conifer trunk if it can't find a suitable cavity; we usually detect it thanks to scolding chickadees. It calls persistently on still nights in spring and early summer, the *toot, toot, toot, toot* call steady and sharp, like a truck's backup signal.

Forehead streaked rather than spotted; few white spots on back except along folded wings.

Common Nighthawk

Chordeiles minor

L 9" | **WS** 21.5"

Once an icon of cities, this nightjar breeds throughout, but has declined dramatically and is now a species of Special Concern; hundreds can still be seen on August evenings moving along Lake Superior. Roosts on the ground, thick branches and wires, flat roofs, or, more rarely, balcony railings and other unexpected spots. In late afternoon and evening takes off in fluttering, erratic flight to capture insects in its huge mouth, its narrow wings occasionally set in a deep V. The *zheeert* call, often described as "peent," is louder and buzzier than the woodcock's flat, quiet *beep*.

Narrow wings have a white crescent near the pointed tip.

Tiny bill and legs; wings extend beyond the tail.

Eastern Whip-poor-will

Antrostomus vociferus

L 9.75" | **WS** 19"

This nightjar, declining throughout its range, breeds locally in mixed and coniferous woods in the north and east. It's more nocturnal than nighthawks and seen far less often. Stiff feathers called rictal bristles, jutting forward below the bill, may be visible on roosting birds. Tail is long with large white corners; folded wings short. In flight, wings are broader than nighthawk's and lack white crescents. The rich, piercing *whip-poor-will!* call, given over and over throughout the night, is thrilling for birders but torture for sleep-deprived campers.

Resembles nighthawk except for bristles at base of bill, shorter wings, and long, white-cornered tail.

Chimney Swift

Chaetura pelagica

L 5.25" | **WS** 14"

This little bird, described by Roger Tory Peterson as a flying cigar, is widespread but declining throughout. Virtually always seen aloft, wing beats are shallow and stiff; during courtship it may raise the wings and tilt side to side in a rocking display. It roosts and nests in chimneys, hollow trees, and towers constructed specifically for swifts. Conservation involves careful counts at summer and fall roosts; dozens or hundreds may swirl in a tornado-shaped stream into a single tower. Exuberant chattering calls attention to swifts in large cities as well as wilderness.

Wings form shallow arcs extending from cigar-shaped body; most wing beats are shallow and stiff.

Ruby-throated Hummingbird

Archilochus colubris

L 3–3.5″ | **WS** 3–4.5″

Our only breeding hummingbird is common and widespread from Mother's Day to Labor Day. Adult male's iridescent throat feathers blackish or brilliant red, depending on angle of light. Female and young have white throat. Sometimes confused with nectar-feeding moths. Attracted to backyards during migration, and may nest wherever spider silk and food are available. Minnesota has records of six other hummingbird species, most in fall after most Ruby-throateds have left. The wings produce the eponymous hum. It also gives soft *tchew* calls, often mixed with chips in an excited chatter.

Adult male's throat color depends on light. Tail black.

Female with white throat, golden-green back, white-tipped tail.

Belted Kingfisher

Megaceryle alcyon

L 12.5″ | **WS** 21″

Our only kingfisher is common throughout from spring through fall and, rarely, in the south in winter. It looks like a bulky, shaggy Blue Jay. Female has rusty flanks and belly band, which male lacks. It sits on a conspicuous perch before taking off in strong, direct flight, suddenly hovering over a promising spot, the body angled so the head faces directly down searching for fish. The feet are ridiculously tiny; small fish are caught and carried in the large, sturdy bill. It excavates its nest in a streamside bank or road cut. The distinctive loud, dry rattle carries a long distance.

Female brighter than male, with rusty flanks and belly band.

Shaggy-crested male has bluish breast band.

Red-headed Woodpecker

Melanerpes erythrocephalus

L 9.25″ | **WS** 17″

This boldly marked woodpecker, declining steadily in recent decades, is an uncommon and local summer resident, mostly associated with oaks. Some are counted every year at Hawk Ridge; a few winter locally in the southeast. Sexes alike, with solid red head, solid white body, and large wing patches that stand out on black wings and tail. Juvenile, often seen in fall, is brown with duller, streaked belly and smaller wing patches. The only other woodpecker with large white wing patches is the gigantic Pileated. The loud *queark!* call is harsher and sharper than that of the Red-bellied Woodpecker.

No streaking on solid red, white, and black plumage.

Immature with streaked underparts, solid brown and white back.

Red-bellied Woodpecker

Melanerpes carolinus

L 9.25″ | **WS** 16″

This strikingly patterned permanent resident, once limited to
the southern half, is increasing in the north, especially near
shade trees and at feeders, where it takes suet, sunflower,
peanuts, jelly, and even sugar water. Black and white horizontal
striping on back in all plumages; juvenile lacks red on head.
Pinkish or reddish area in the center of the belly is usually
concealed. In flight, white rump and tail and white wing
crescents are conspicuous. Red-bellied calls frequently, giving
a distinctive *chi-chi-chi-chi*; the *quirr* call is softer than the
similar call of Red-headed.

Brilliant red nape extends to the forehead
in adult male.

Red nape, gray crown in this adult female.
Juvenile's head would be all brown.

Yellow-bellied Sapsucker

Sphyrapicus varius

L 7–8.75" | **WS** 13.5–16"

This common resident from late March through October shows
a vertical white stripe on the dark wing in all plumages. Adult
male has red throat; both sexes have red forehead. Juvenile (seen after early summer) is brown and scruffy-looking,
without strong facial markings. Digs tiny holes in horizontal
rows in a variety of trees, especially aspens, for sap and the
insects attracted to it. These holes also attract hummingbirds
and small insectivores, especially on cold spring mornings
when food is scarce. The loud drum is slow and syncopated. The
call is a whiny, catbird-like descending *mew*.

Male, peeking out of
hole, has red throat;
female has white throat.

Downy Woodpecker

Dryobates pubescens

L 6″ | **WS** 11″

Our tiniest, most widespread woodpecker is seen year-round
in weeds, shrubs, and trees, and visits feeders for sunflower,
suet, jelly, and sugar water. Like the Hairy, has a solid white
back; adult male has a bright red spot on the nape, which adult
female lacks, and juvenile has a dull red forehead. The Downy's
smaller size is obvious when side by side with Hairy. Unlike the
Hairy, the Downy's bill is shorter than the head and the white
outer tail feathers have black spots, sometimes easy to see. The
pik call is soft and dull; rattle call descends in pitch. Drumming
is fast and steady.

Short bill, black spots on
outer tail, no red on female.

The red nape spot
identifies males.

Hairy Woodpecker

Dryobates villosus

L 8.5″ | **WS** 14.5″

This common and widespread permanent resident is more limited to treed habitats than the very similar Downy. The Hairy has a proportionally longer bill (almost as long as the head) and pure white or lightly stained outer tail feathers without black spots. It visits feeders for suet and peanut butter, less often for other fare. Like the Downy, adult male has a red nape spot; juvenile has a red forehead. The call, a sharp *peek!*, is louder and sharper than the Downy's *pik*; sputtering rattle notes are usually all on the same pitch. The steady drum is even more rapid than that of the Downy.

Bill about as long as the head; no black on outer tail.

Long bill; no red on adult female.

American Three-toed Woodpecker

Picoides dorsalis

L 8″ **WS** 15″

This very rare permanent resident of the forested north is very hard to see, but in some winters may frequent feeding stations in the Sax-Zim Bog. Unlike the less rare Black-backed Woodpecker, the Three-toed has some whitish on the back; both have distinctive black and white barring on the sides. Juvenile and adult male have a yellow forehead. It scrapes and taps to pull bark off dead trees, often with Black-backeds, especially in burned-over tracts. Sounds are similar to Downy; the main call is a flatter, more wooden-toned *pwik*. Rattle call doesn't descend. Drum rapid and steady.

Male and juvenile have yellow forehead.

Barring on sides usually conspicuous; some white on back.

Black-backed Woodpecker

Picoides arcticus

L 9" | **WS** 16"

This uncommon permanent resident and irruptive winter
visitor of the forested north is eagerly sought by birders in
northern Minnesota every winter. Like the Three-toed, it's shy
and retiring and flakes bark off dead and dying trees, especially
in burnt or cut-over areas, but is more common, frequenting the
Sax-Zim Bog more reliably. Like the Three-toed, the underparts
are strongly barred, and male and juvenile have yellow forehead; unlike that species, the Black-backed's back and wings
are solid black. The call is a strident *chuck*, often followed by
an odd squeaky rattle. Drumming is steady and rapid.

Solid black back. Male and juvenile
have yellow forehead.

Strongly barred sides; adult female has
black forehead.

Northern Flicker

Colaptes auratus

L 11.5″ | **WS** 18″

This widespread resident from April through October is
uncommon in winter, mostly in the south and especially near
the Twin Cities. It has a black bib, brown back with black bars,
and spotted underparts. Adult has a red crescent on the nape;
adult male and juveniles have black mustache mark. In flight,
the large white rump is conspicuous from behind and yellow
wing and tail linings from below. It's found less at feeders and
more on the ground than other backyard woodpeckers, feeding
on ants. Rapid drumming and the *wicka wicka wicka* call are
given during breeding, the sharp *keeer* call anytime.

Adult female, peeking out of hole, lacks
mustache.

No white on wings; yellow wings and
tail visible from below.

Pileated Woodpecker

Dryocopus pileatus

L 17.5″ | **WS** 27.5″

This enormous woodpecker, common except in prairie and agricultural areas of the west and south, feeds on ants and wood-boring beetles in and beneath decaying trees and logs; it also sometimes feeds in small branches of aspens or various berry shrubs and trees, and sometimes visits suet feeders. Male has a red mustache and forehead; female's are black. In flight, white patches on the wings and powerful irregular wing beats distinguish them from crows. The yelling call, *kek kek kek kek*, is loud and arresting. The drumming is steady, loud, and slower than in most woodpeckers.

Large, with red crest; female has a black forehead and mustache. In flight across roads and other open areas, flight is direct, the wings rowing through the air more powerfully than crows; the big white wing patches are distinctive.

American Kestrel

Falco sparverius

L 9.5" | **WS** 22"

This tiny, red-tailed falcon breeds in dwindling numbers throughout, nesting in cavities in open areas with scattered trees; some winter in the south. The main migration at Hawk Ridge is concentrated on August and September days when dragonflies are aloft. Male has steel-blue wings; female and juvenile are brown. Frequently seen on power lines, it's bigger-headed and more hunched up than a Mourning Dove. It often hovers in one spot, pointed wings beating steadily. Delicate in flight; bobs tail when alighting. The distinctive strident *killy-killy-killy* call is most often given while nesting.

Narrow, pointed wings with a row of spots along the trailing edge help identify flying birds from below. Flight is buoyant.

Merlin
Falco columbarius

L 10.5″ | **WS** 29″

This tiny dynamo nests in increasing numbers in forests, towns, and cities of the north; a few winter here and there throughout. At Hawk Ridge, it often dive bombs owl decoys; its migration peaks from September through mid-October. Darker and less colorful than kestrels, but the Merlin is only an inch longer, with relatively short tail and wings, and weighs 40 percent more, giving it speed and power to chase and capture birds as large as pigeons. Its wing beats are shallow and rapid. Surprisingly noisy for a bird of prey, its loud, rapid, trilling cries sound like a hyperactive Killdeer.

Dark eyes, unlike accipiters; more slender than Broad-winged.

All dark; wing beats more powerful than Kestrel's.

Peregrine Falcon

Falco peregrinus

L 16.5" | **WS** 41"

This muscular falcon, once critically endangered, is increasing due to reintroduction programs; now found year-round in wetlands, open areas, and cities. In flight, adult's pale throat and upper breast form a "headlight." The extremely rare Prairie Falcon and Gyrfalcon appear now and then; both have a narrower sideburn mark. From beneath in flight, Peregrine has fairly uniform wings; paler Prairie has dark contrasting "wing-pits," and gray Gyrfalcon (the color we usually see) has pale wings with somewhat darker, contrasting underwing coverts. Peregrine's call is loud and screechy, but low-pitched.

Wings thick at body, tapering to a point; long tail tapered.

Adult has thick black sideburns, white throat and breast.

Olive-sided Flycatcher

Contopus cooperi

L 7–8″ | **WS** 12.9″

This dark, oversized pewee is an uncommon breeder in the
forested and boggy northeast, and can appear anywhere in
May or during its early fall migration from August through
the first half of September. It seems to be wearing a dark olive
vest that it can't quite close in the front over its whitish long
underwear. From behind, two large cottony patches of white on
the flanks are sometimes noticeable on adults. It is usually seen
on conspicuous high perches such as snags, both on territory
and during migration, seldom lurking in dense branches. Its
distinctive loud song is a piercing *Quick! Three beers!*

Head dark; no eye ring, and
the bill is mostly dark. Dark
olive sides, white along
center of breast and belly.

Eastern Wood-Pewee

Contopus virens

L 5.5-6.25" | **WS** 10"

Much more common and widespread than the larger Olive-sided Flycatcher, this summer resident arrives in May to breed in hardwood and mixed forests throughout. Like the Olive-sided, it has dusky sides, white wing bars, and a large, dark head with no eye ring. Unlike that species, the pewee has a pale lower bill and never has puffy white patches on the back. It's far more likely in late September than the Olive-sided. Far more often heard than seen. Clear, plaintive *Peee-o-weeee?* is often answered by a descending *Peee-yo*. The *per-wee* call of Yellow-bellied Flycatchers is similar in quality.

Wing bars, soft gray sides, no eye ring, and yellow lower bill help distinguish from similar flycatchers.

Yellow-bellied Flycatcher

Empidonax flaviventris

L 5-6″ | **WS** 7-8″

Flycatchers in this genus ("empids") have wing bars, an eye ring and, usually, a yellow lower mandible; identification is easiest by voice. This uncommon species of northeastern coniferous forests arrives in May and sings through June or early July; after that it's hard to detect, though it remains until September. It's greenish overall with a fairly bright yellow belly. Two calls, each similar to another species. The *je-bunk* is softer and given less often than the Least's more emphatic *che-BEK!* The plaintive *Per-wee?* is shorter than the Wood-Pewee's questioning *Peee-o-weeee?* and never answered.

Yellowish throat, dark beneath with bright yellow belly feathers peeking through; overall more greenish than other empids.

Acadian Flycatcher

Empidonax virescens

L 5.75″ | **WS** 9″

This empid, a species of Special Concern, is uncommon and local in the southeast up through the Twin Cities, breeding mostly in mature forests. It would never be expected in the north. It's more yellowish than other empids except the Yellow-bellied, which is not found in the south except during migration. Like the Yellow-bellied, it's greenish on the back, but has paler underparts, especially on throat. Like other empids, it's usually best identified by the call, a quick, emphatic *Pete's UP,* often interspersed with a rapid, rolling *ti ti ti ti ti.*

Typical empid with wing bars and eye ring. Throat more whitish than the Yellow-bellied's, underparts less yellow.

Alder Flycatcher

Empidonax alnorum

L 6" | **WS** 8.5"

This common resident of the northern two thirds, present from mid-May to mid-September, is darker, with a subtler eye ring, than other empids except for the almost identical Willow. Once considered the same species, these two were split on the basis of song and nesting habitat: the Alder sings in brushy swamps and meadows from late May through early July. The song, sung on territory, is a bouncy, burry *fee-bee´-o*, as if asking for *free BEER*. At any time, it gives a loud, fairly high and musical *pip* call, and a *whit!* call that is higher than the Willow's similar note.

In most lights, the back appears olive. The pale throat contrasts strongly with the dark face; the eye ring is subtle.

Willow Flycatcher

Empidonax traillii

L 6″ | **WS** 8.5″

This flycatcher of brushy habitats in the south and west looks nearly identical to the Alder Flycatcher. During nesting, the two species overlap only in the northwest, where Willows gravitate to wetter, more open areas with some willows, and Alders head to groves with other trees. Unlike most empids, Willow Flycatchers occasionally sing on migration as well as on the breeding grounds. The song, a snappy, wheezy *witch brew!* is less bouncy and more burry than the Alder's song, the two syllables equally emphasized. The *whit!* call is lower and breathier than the Alder's.

Similar to Alder. Tail-flicking habit and brushy habitat help distinguish it from any wood-pewees with a hint of an eye ring.

Least Flycatcher
Empidonax minimus

L 5.25″ | **WS** 7.75″

Our tiniest, most abundant, most frequently noticed empid breeds in deciduous and mixed woods throughout; it's the first empid to arrive, at the beginning of May or even in late April, and the last to leave, at the end of September. Its relatively short bill and short wings give it a compact, big-headed look, and it has the boldest eye ring of our empids. It may have a yellowish wash beneath, never as pronounced as Yellow-bellied's. Extremely vocal during spring migration, it frequently calls out *che-BEK, che-BEK, che-BEK!* in a series. The quick *whit!* call is often given in a series, too.

By far our most common empid. The eye ring and wing bars are pronounced; virtually no yellow anywhere.

Eastern Phoebe

Sayornis phoebe

L 5.5-6.5″ | **WS** 10-11″

This common resident throughout arrives in March, long before other flycatchers, and some remain as late as November. Dark-headed, without eye rings; lacks wing bars, though pale edges of fresh wing feathers in fall can resemble wing bars. Continuously bobs tail up and down. Say's Phoebe, a rare migrant and summer visitor, is darker overall (including throat and breast) with an orangey lower belly; it also pumps its tail. In spring, it sings persistently at dawn and on and off through the day, alternating a raspy *FEE-BEE!* with a sweeter *fee-bee bee*; the song is not whistled. Also gives a *chip!*

Overall dark, the head slightly darker than the back, wings, and sides; creamy underparts may have a yellowish tinge.

Great Crested Flycatcher
Myiarchus crinitus

L 8.75" | **WS** 13"

Named for its shaggy head, this robust flycatcher breeds
throughout except for the far northeast. Brown head and back;
gray breast contrasts with bright yellow belly. The primary
wing feathers and underside of the tail are rusty. It usually
forages for insects and berries within the foliage of trees. It
nests in cavities, including bird boxes. Twice in late fall, a
similar flycatcher with a pale belly and solid black bill has
turned up and been identified as an Ash-throated Flycatcher
from the American Southwest. Gives frequent piercing *wheep!*
and raspy *prrreeep, prrreeep, prreeep* calls.

Shaggy head, yellow
belly meeting gray
breast, and rusty
feathers in the
wings and tail;
mostly dark bill.

Western Kingbird

Tyrannus verticalis

L 8–9.5" | **WS** 14.5–15.75"

This broad-shouldered tyrant of prairies and open habitat can be common in summer in the west and sometimes near the Mississippi; it pops up elsewhere during migration, but is far rarer here than the Eastern Kingbird. Like the Eastern and the Scissor-tailed Flycatcher, it sits on wires, fences, and other conspicuous perches in open habitat. Pale gray head and breast, olive back, darker wings, yellow belly, and black tail with white outer tail feathers identify this species. Aggressive attacks on larger birds, including hawks and eagles, give it its name. It gives squeaky, sputtering calls.

Broad-shouldered; soft gray head and breast, yellow belly.

Shallow wing beats; white-edged tail.

Eastern Kingbird
Tyrannus tyrannus

L 9" | **WS** 15"

This common summer resident breeds throughout. Solid black face and crown and very dark gray wings and back. Pure white beneath, square black tail with white tip. A line of red feathers on the crown of a peeved or territorial male is usually hidden. Sits conspicuously on fences, wires, and bare branches, fluttering up on characteristically stiff, shallow wing beats to grab insects in midair or chase off perceived enemies; can successfully drive off a Bald Eagle from its territory. The song is a distinctive series of scratchy and thin, but energetically zippy, sputtering notes.

Two-toned dark and white; broad-shouldered, macho stance.

From behind, white tail tip conspicuous.

Scissor-tailed Flycatcher

Tyrannus forficatus

L 8.5–14.5″ | **WS** 14.5″

This astonishingly lithe, graceful kingbird is a rare and unpredictable visitor. When one shows up, it prefers conspicuous perches in open areas. The soft silver-gray head and body contrast with dark wings, and the reddish pink at the bend of the wing and peachy flanks add a splash of color. Tail feathers are exceptionally long, especially in adult male; they flare outward to form two rounded tips. The far rarer Fork-tailed Flycatcher has a black crown and face and blacker wings; the extremely long tail feathers taper to form two points. Sputtery calls are lower-pitched than Western Kingbird's.

When one appears in Minnesota, it's easily recognized by its soft gray head and back and extraordinary tail.

Northern Shrike

Lanius borealis

L 8.5″　|　**WS** 12″

This uncommon but widespread winter visitor throughout has a narrow black facial mask, bordered with white near the eye, and a light gray crown; its underparts are subtly barred. A predatory songbird, it hunts for rodents and small birds from wires, fences, or spires of trees. It impales its prey on thorns and barbed wire, returning to its caches when hungry. The Loggerhead Shrike, designated Endangered here, breeds locally in the west and south and is never found in winter; its black mask connects in the center, its crown and back are darker gray, and its pale underparts are never barred.

Narrow mask; light gray forehead, subtly barred breast.

Yellow-throated Vireo

Vireo flavifrons

L 5.5" | **WS** 9.5"

Vireos resemble warblers but have a thicker, hooked bill. This one, beefier than most warblers, breeds in mature deciduous forests except in the southwest and far northeast. Its bright yellow throat and breast, white belly and sides, and bold white wing bars on dark wings are superficially similar to Pine Warbler, but yellow spectacles and thicker, hooked bill much different. It stays in the middle and upper levels of large, thick trees, but its persistent singing makes it easy to detect. The song is a series of low, burry 2- and 3-note phrases with the tonal quality of a Scarlet Tanager's.

Bright yellow spectacles, throat, and breast; white wing bars; white flanks and lower belly; thick bill.

Blue-headed Vireo

Vireo solitarius

L 5.5″ | **WS** 9.5″

One of the first insectivores to return to northern forests in spring, the Blue-headed Vireo is a fairly common migrant throughout and breeds in northern forests. Conspicuous white spectacles on the steel blue head and bright white throat are unique; wing bars and yellowish flanks are also seen on the extremely rare White-eyed. Not as persistent a singer in June and early July as other vireos, but often forages at eye level. Its song is a series of short phrases, delivered more slowly than Red-eyed Vireo phrases. The phrases have a richer, sweeter quality than those of Red-eyeds, with an occasional burry phrase thrown in.

White spectacles and wing bars, yellowish flanks.

Dark head, yellow flanks; pure white throat and breast.

Warbling Vireo

Vireo gilvus

L 4.5" | **WS** 8.75"

Our most nondescript vireo is common in summer throughout the state, except for the far northeast, in large trees, especially aspens and cottonwoods, near water. Most noteworthy for its lack of field marks: a faint eye line, no wing bars, pale beneath with a subtle wash of yellow, throat whitish. Sings persistently from early May until July. Its song sounds like rushed and nonsensical run-on sentences: *veedo veedee, veedo veedee, veedo veedee, VEET?* Males sometimes sing while incubating eggs. The loud, raspy call notes, whiny and complaining, are given frequently until it leaves in September.

Very low contrast; dull eye line, no wing bars.

Frequently gives complaining call notes.

Philadelphia Vireo

Vireo philadelphicus

L 5.25" | **WS** 8"

This rare breeder in the northeast looks a bit like the much more widespread Warbling Vireo and sings like the much more common Red-eyed Vireo; neither has its soft yellowish throat and breast. The dark lores on the otherwise drab face give it the look of a Warbling Vireo wearing a touch of eye makeup. The song is composed of short robin-like phrases given every three seconds on average. Even experts have trouble distinguishing the song from the Red-eyed Vireo's; it averages a bit softer and higher-pitched, with longer intervals between the short phrases.

Very low contrast like Warbling, but tapering dark eye line and yellow center of the throat.

Red-eyed Vireo

Vireo olivaceus

L 6" **WS** 10"

This common resident is found from May through September in
a wide variety of forests, woodlands, and suburbs throughout.
Eye line and cap are much more pronounced than on Warbling
or Philadelphia, and the gray crown is edged with black. May
have a yellowish wash at the bend of the wing, but the throat
and belly are always white. Our most persistent singer gives an
endless stream of robin-like phrases all day and all summer,
even into September. This is also one of the first species to
notice small owls and other dangers; it complains about every
irritation with a whiny, raspy call.

Plain olive back and wings, white beneath,
flat gray crown. White eyebrow bordered
by dark eye line and dark edge to crown.

Canada Jay
Perisoreus canadensis

L 11" | **WS** 18"

This permanent resident of northern bogs and forests looks like a chickadee on steroids and acts like the Artful Dodger, following large mammals, including birders, on ghost-like silent wings. It feeds on meat, including eggs and nestlings of other species; in spring and summer, it's hard to find one not being chased by small songbirds. Juvenile, hatched in late winter, is sooty grayish brown. Clark's Nutcracker, an extremely rare visitor, is sleeker, has a longer bill, black wings, and white patches in wings and tail. Near people, this jay gives a variety of quiet whistled or husky calls.

Fluffy gray. Big head with large eyes, long rounded tail.

Juvenile is sooty gray, the size and shape of adult.

Blue Jay

Cyanocitta cristata

L 11″ | **WS** 16″

Our only crested jay, with strikingly complex plumage patterns, is found year-round throughout the state, but many migrate; on some September days, a thousand or more are tallied at Hawk Ridge. The shape in flight—rounded wings and long tail—is superficially like accipiters, but Blue Jay has a long bill, flaps without soaring, shows much more white underneath, and migrates in large flocks. Squawking noisily at any sign of danger, this jay alerts us to owls on daytime roosts. It gives a wide variety of calls, some bell-like or whispery, in addition to the loud *jay-jay* squawks.

No other Minnesota bird has blue plumage and a crest. The crest may be lowered, especially around family or flock members.

American Crow

Corvus brachyrhynchos

L 18.5" | **WS** 36.5"

This noisy, intelligent, sociable, oversized songbird is found year-round throughout the state in virtually every habitat; many retreat from northern areas in winter even as others remain. A Minnesota birder's first sign of spring is a crow carrying a stick. Unlike blackbirds, you can count a crow's wing beats, and unlike ravens, a crow seldom soars except when coming in for a landing. The tail feathers are the same length, making the end of the tail appear even whether it's fanned or closed. Adult gives a raspy *caw caw* as well as a variety of other sounds, some surprisingly soft and musical.

Tail is blunt-tipped, wings rounded.

Bill straight, forehead low and flat, throat feathers sleek.

Common Raven

Corvus corax

L 24.5" | **WS** 46"

The largest songbird on earth is a permanent resident in the north, less common elsewhere. It's regularly seen on migration from Hawk Ridge, but its numbers never seem to increase south of there. Much larger and heavier than a crow, with shaggy throat feathers. The wings are relatively longer and more pointed. The tail appears pointed because the central feathers are longer than the outer ones. Ravens are far more likely than crows to soar and engage in aerial acrobatics. Calls include various croaks and a large repertoire of other sounds, but none would be called "caws."

Pointed tail. Wings seem a bit long and pointed.

Massive bill is slightly curved; the forehead is steep.

Black-billed Magpie

Pica hudsonia

L 20.5″ | **WS** 23.5″

This long-tailed crow relative is a permanent northern resident, especially in aspen parklands in the northwest; the small
population in the Sax-Zim Bog and Floodwood is among the
easternmost on the continent. Black wing and tail feathers
are iridescent, and can appear purple or greenish. The magpie
is fairly easy to recognize in flight because of the large white
patches on the wings and body and enormous tail. Like its crow
and jay relatives, the magpie is very vocal, giving a querulous,
chattering *queg-queg-queg-queg*, a Blue Jay-like ascending call,
and various raspy chattering sounds.

Juvenile has shorter tail, red at
gape of bill.

Black and white pattern;
long, tapered tail.

Horned Lark
Eremophila alpestris

L 7″ **WS** 12.5″

This bird of barren or plowed fields and prairies is most abundant in the south and west, but can appear anywhere in migration, especially along Lake Superior in fall. It often over-winters in mixed flocks with longspurs and Snow Buntings, especially southwest. Amount of yellow on black and white face varies. Juvenile lacks the distinctive black breast and facial markings of adult. In flight, the black tail is distinctive. It runs and walks rather than hops, and is much more often found on the ground than perched in trees and shrubs. Calls and flight song are delicate and tinkling.

Brown upperparts often blend with ground. Pale underparts, slender but sturdy bill, bold face pattern, black tail.

Purple Martin

Progne subis

L 8″ | **WS** 16″

Our largest swallow, designated Special Concern, is widespread but rare in the northeast. It arrives in late April (one or two may appear earlier) and disappears in September. Male is the only completely dark swallow; dusky, nondescript female looks like oversized Rough-winged Swallow. More muscular than other swallows, flies more slowly and often soars with wings and notched tail spread. Guidelines to help martins are available from the Purple Martin Conservation Association. Rich, gurgling warbles and whistles and low *churr* calls provide an endlessly pleasing soundtrack near any nesting colony.

Iridescent purple male can appear all black.

Often soars on broad, pointed wings; body is heavy.

Tree Swallow

Tachycineta bicolor

L 5.25" | **WS** 13"

This common, widespread summer resident is the first swallow to arrive in March and the only one entirely snow-white beneath, from the throat to beneath the notched tail. Brownish-backed juvenile may have diffuse dusky breast band. Nests in bluebird boxes, woodpecker holes, and natural cavities in snags near water. An adult's white underparts may extend above the flanks to the sides of the rump, making optimistic birders think of the exceedingly rare Violet-green Swallow. The pleasing twitters, chirps, gurgles, and clicking calls Tree Swallows make sound like spring itself.

Iridescent green or blue above, underparts pure white.

Tree Swallow often glides in flight. Juvenile brown-backed.

Northern Rough-winged Swallow

Stelgidopteryx serripennis

L 5″ | **WS** 11″

Our most nondescript swallow is a common breeder throughout, only locally in the northeast. The plumage is dull brown above and lighter brown from the throat to the paler belly, like a miniature female Purple Martin. It's named for tiny hooked barbs along the primary wing feathers, which feel raspy to the touch but are impossible to see in the field. Flight not as rapid as Bank Swallow. Pair tunnels into riverbank or road cut to nest; they do not form colonies. The low, dry *brrt* calls give the impression of irritableness.

Brown and nondescript. When perched, the breast seems more puffed out than other swallows. Tail notched.

Bank Swallow

Riparia riparia

L 5″ | **WS** 10.5″

Our tiniest swallow breeds in colonies throughout, in natural banks and sand piles at large construction sites. It's brown-backed like the somewhat larger Rough-winged Swallow, but with a subtly paler rump. The clean dark band across the breast widens at the sides. Juvenile Tree Swallow may have a much more diffuse band. The wing beats are quick, flight rapid and direct. Skittish, and reluctant to return to nest under observation, so pull back if birds are flying out but not coming back. The harsh, rapid twitters sound cranky; they're higher and more chattering than the Rough-winged.

Tiny, fast flier. No other Minnesota swallow has a white throat and clean, well-defined breast band.

Cliff Swallow

Petrochelidon pyrrhonota

L 5" | **WS** 11.5"

This extremely sociable swallow breeds in colonies throughout, often under eaves and bridges, in little gourd-shaped "adobe houses"; when one peeks out of the round entrance hole, its pale forehead gleams in the dark. It often nests near Barn Swallow, which also has a rusty throat and creamy breast; the two often gather in squabbling groups at the same mud puddles to pick up nest materials. The "headlight" on the forehead, pale rump, squared tail, and shape of the nest easily separate this from the Barn. Cliff Swallows make cheerful-sounding, conversational squeaks and purring notes.

Creamy forehead gleams like a headlight from dark nest. Tail squared. Large buffy or rusty rump patch.

Barn Swallow

Hirundo rustica

L 6.5" | **WS** 12"

This swallow with the lithe body and elegant "swallowtail"
breeds throughout, often on eaves, in barns, or under bridges.
It arrives soon after Tree Swallow in spring, and can be seen
in September after other swallows have vanished for the year.
Our only fork-tailed swallow's all-dark face and rump quickly
distinguish it from the Cliff Swallow. Flight is rapid and
graceful. Its heavy mud nest is a cup, open on the top rather than
the side. The twittering calls and squeaky buzzes are pleasing to
hear unless the bird is dive-bombing you near its nest.

Dark blue above, cream
and rusty below, dark
forehead and rump, deeply
forked tail. May have a thin
blue line across breast.

Black-capped Chickadee

Poecile atricapillus

L 5-6″ | **WS** 6.25-8.25″

This cheeky acrobat, the size, shape, and bounciness of a ping pong ball with a spiky tail, is a common permanent resident throughout; it should serve as our emergency auxiliary state bird after loons have flown the coop for winter. The long narrow tail, tiny round body, and bouncy flight make it easy to recognize. It attracts many small migrant and wintering songbirds, so a chickadee flock can signal the presence of other interesting species, too. Gives *chickadee-dee-dee* calls and gargles. Males sing a pure, whistled *Hey, sweetie!* song even in the dead of winter.

White cheeks, buffy sides, "frosted" wings, and black bib. The gray back contrasts sharply with the black cap.

Boreal Chickadee

Poecile hudsonicus

L 4.75–5.5" | **WS** 8"

This year-round resident of northern coniferous forests is most easily seen in the Sax-Zim Bog. Occasionally wanders in winter, when it's attracted to peanut butter more than other feeder offerings. Like a quieter, less sociable Black-capped, but with much darker plumage and a smaller, duskier cheek patch. From high in a dense conifer, when the tail isn't visible, the dark back makes it easy to mistake for a Red-breasted Nuthatch. The soft, wheezy *chick-a-dee* call sounds like a Black-capped with a tragic disease. In late winter is often heard making a warbling jumble of wheezy notes.

The brown cap blends into the mostly brown back. Small cheek patch edged with gray, sides brownish orange.

Tufted Titmouse

Baeolophus bicolor

L 6.5″ | **WS** 9.5″

One of the hardest of our permanent resident birds to see in the state except at a staked-out feeder, this small crested bird is rare and local in the southeast corner. Gray above, whitish face and underparts with orange flanks, a distinctive black mark between the large eyes. It has the same acrobatic habits as a chickadee. Wintering flock is made up of a pair or family, and may loosely associate with chickadee flocks. Song is a clear whistled *peter-peter-peter* given several times in quick succession; also gives a scratchy, chickadee-like *tsee-day-day-day* and several scolding notes.

Sturdy black bill. Evenly gray above with a whitish face and underparts, black mark above bill, orange flanks.

Red-breasted Nuthatch

Sitta canadensis

L 4.25" | **WS** 7.5"

This topsy-turvy resident of coniferous forests is widespread during migration and winter, especially in "irruptive years." The back is solid bluish-gray; belly rusty, with at least a rusty wash on breast. The fairly long bill is black; the upper mandible is straight, the lower angled up. In flight, the tiny, thick body and short tail are distinctive. Visits feeders for sunflower, suet, peanuts, and peanut butter. Year-round, it's usually found in small groups, often with chickadees. Gives rapid beeps and *whaa! whaa! whaa!* "tiny tin horn" calls, all sounding plaintive and whiny.

Male's cap black; white above and below eye line.

Female like male, but cap matches the dark back.

White-breasted Nuthatch

Sitta carolinensis

L 5.25″ | **WS** 9.25″

This permanent resident, least common in the northeast, is associated with deciduous woods. The jet-black nape contrasts with the bluish-gray back; the male's crown matches the nape, the female's matches the back. It visits feeders for sunflower, suet, and nuts. Usually standoffish, it stays on the outskirts of the activity even when with a chickadee flock, foraging by working its way up, down, and around tree trunks and large limbs. The *yank yank* calls sound irritable and cranky rather than whiny. The song, heard mostly in late winter and spring, is a rapid series of identical *yah yah* notes.

White cheek and underparts, rusty flanks. Male's crown black.

Black eye stands out on white face. Female's crown dark gray.

Brown Creeper

Certhia americana

L 5" | **WS** 7.25"

This common resident breeds in forests in the northeast and migrates throughout; some winter here. Mottled brown and white above, white beneath; the slender bill and stiff tail feathers curve downward. It seems earnest as it spirals steadily up a tree trunk and then drops to the next tree to spiral up again, usually keeping to itself. Rarely visits suet feeders. The extremely high-pitched *seee* calls, similar to those of Golden-crowned Kinglets, can sound piercing to young ears; many older birders can't hear them. The song is a simple, steady series of similar high-frequency lisping tones.

The creeper's tail and long claws help support it against vertical tree trunks. The plumage is subtly beautiful.

House Wren

Troglodytes aedon

L 4.75" | **WS** 6"

Arriving in April or early May, this active, bold little insectivore breeds throughout except in deep woods, often in backyards. The entire body is brown. The face is plain, with no eyebrow; the wings and tail are distinctly barred. Each male builds multiple stick nests inside cavities, birdhouses, and nooks and crannies; it can be hard to know which was actually chosen by the female unless you see adults delivering food to the brood. Nesting can continue into August. The bubbly song is a rapid, exuberant jumble of rich notes. It also gives harsh scolding notes and rattles.

Softer brown above and overall lighter than Winter Wren, with a longer tail. Fine barring on wings and tail.

Winter Wren
Troglodytes hiemalis

L 3.5" | **WS** 4.75–6.25"

This dark, diminutive skulker breeds throughout the northern coniferous forest and locally in forests along the St. Croix and Mississippi Rivers, arriving earlier in spring and leaving in fall after House Wrens. It actively flits about within the roots of fallen trees, in crevices under rocks, and other tiny spaces, usually unobserved. It seldom sings away from its breeding grounds. The delicate yet exuberant "silver-threaded" song consists of a jumble of tinkling notes lasting 8 seconds or more. Learning the *chup chup* call notes helps us notice migrating or rare overwintering birds.

Darker than the similar House Wren; it usually holds its very short tail cocked up, and has a fairly noticeable eyebrow.

Sedge Wren

Cistothorus stellaris

L 4–5" | **WS** 6"

This common and widespread little wren breeds in wet meadows and pastures throughout the state. Delicate streaks on the crown are never present on the similar Marsh Wren. It can be frustratingly difficult to see, even when it's singing from an exposed stalk, until it takes off. Its direct, smooth flight on tiny wings just above the vegetation makes it look like an oversized bumblebee; careful tracking can reveal it on its next perch. The song is twangy, starting with a few sharp *chip* notes and breaking into a rapid sputtering chatter; the entire body quivers with the effort.

Overall buffy, with fairly conspicuous white streaking on the back and delicate streaking on the crown.

Marsh Wren

Cistothorus palustris

L 4.75" | **WS** 6.75"

This common little wren breeds in cattail marshes throughout
the state except for the northeast. It investigates every little
thing, yet usually manages to stay hidden in plain sight even
as it scolds us. Buffy beneath like the Sedge Wren, it's usually
brighter chestnut above, and its dark crown is never streaked. A
persistent vocalist night and day, it produces a gurgling, rattling
trill that sounds like an old-fashioned treadle sewing machine.
Its fairly loud *chek chek, chek chek chek* calls, sometimes punctuated with thin gurgling notes, are distinctive, too.

Overall darker than Sedge Wren, with a
darker, more uniform cap, and a more
pronounced eyebrow and eye line.

Carolina Wren

Thryothorus ludovicianus

L 5″ | **WS** 7″

Consider yourself lucky if you see this oversized wren in Minnesota; it's rare and unpredictable in all seasons, but occasionally breeds in the southeast. When present, it's noisy, often found in backyards, and may stick around for days after a rare bird alert goes out. Rich brown above, buffy below, with a pronounced white eyebrow; wings and tail finely barred. The song, a surprisingly loud *teakettle teakettle teakettle*, is similar to that of a Tufted Titmouse but with a more brilliant, ringing quality. It also gives a wide variety of raspy, chattery, and cheery calls.

Deep reddish brown above, soft orangey below. Subtle barring on wings and tail, pronounced white eyebrow.

Blue-gray Gnatcatcher

Polioptila caerulea

L 4" | **WS** 6.25"

Once very local in the state, this tiny, slender bird is now
common and regular in mature deciduous woods of the southeast; it makes occasional appearances elsewhere. Soft bluish
above, pure white beneath. Breeding male has a black forehead
mark just above its eyes that makes it seem comically judg-
mental. Flitting about, flicking its long tail from side to side as
it searches for insects at all heights in trees and shrubs, it could
make a chickadee seem sluggish. The song is a soft and high
jumble of notes including *spzee* calls and weird, soft imitations
of other species.

White outer
feathers edge the
long black tail.

Breeding male has
black forehead mark.

Golden-crowned Kinglet

Regulus satrapa

L 3.75" | **WS** 6.25"

This exceptionally hardy sprite breeds in the coniferous forests, migrates throughout, and winters here and there—surprising for a tiny insectivore that virtually never visits feeders but usually stays high in spruces and firs. The tapered eye line looks like carefully applied eyeliner. Male has bright red feathers in the golden crown. Has a restless habit of flicking its wings every second or two. The extremely high-pitched call notes and song are similar to those of Brown Creepers, but the kinglet often gives the call notes in quick triplets: *see-see-see*.

Golden crown encircled by black; subtle tapered eye line.

Male's crown feathers red and golden, raised when agitated.

Ruby-crowned Kinglet

Corthylio calendula

L 4″ | **WS** 6.75″

This tiny kinglet is a common migrant throughout and breeds in the northeast. Similar to Golden-crowned from the neck down, it also flicks its wings, but rather than an eye line, it has an eye ring, and female and juvenile lack bright crown feathers; adult male conceals them unless displaying. Both kinglets arrive in late March or April. Ruby-crowned visits deciduous trees and shrubs as well as conifers. The song starts with a few high-pitched, lisping notes and then breaks into a rich warbling jumble of notes with a few triplets, like *liberty liberty liberty*. Calls sound irritable and scolding.

Eye ring, single wing bar; wing feathers edged with yellow.

Displaying male's exposed crown vivid red.

Eastern Bluebird

Sialia sialis

L 7" | **WS** 13"

This red, white, and blue bird is common in open areas and forest clearings beginning in March; some winter. Except on territory, seen in flocks, especially in fruit trees in fall. Hunts from a perch, fluttering down to grab prey. Increasing numbers are due in large part to people setting out nest boxes. Very rarely, a Mountain Bluebird turns up in the state; male has a blue breast, female is dusky gray with pale blue wings and tail. Eastern has a rich, warm warbled song of several 1- to 3-note phrases, with some harsher 2-note chattering phrases mixed in. The call is a soft, musical *toodle-ee.*

Male is vivid blue above; rusty breast and white belly.

Fledgling is spotted, with a bit of blue on wings and tail.

Townsend's Solitaire

Myadestes townsendi

L 8.25″ | **WS** 13.25″

This rare visitor from western states is the picture of subdued elegance when it is discovered in a fruit tree during migration or winter; one often turns up in a mountain ash in Duluth or along the North Shore in winter, usually keeping to itself rather than joining a flock of robins or waxwings. The soft wing pattern is subtle, but distinguishes it from the dullest female bluebirds or other thrushes. We seldom hear the rich, warbled territorial song here, but occasionally a winter visitor gives the clear, ringing *too* call.

Soft gray body with white eye ring, white outer tail feathers, and pretty but subtle buffy pattern on wings.

Veery
Catharus fuscescens

L 7" | **WS** 12"

Four similar thrushes of the genus *Catharus* can be seen anywhere here during migration. The Veery breeds widely in the east and north, especially in moist forests. It usually skulks in the shadows, but especially during migration sometimes hops robin-like on wooded pathways. It has one of the most beautiful and distinctive songs of any bird, often described as water spiraling down a tube. Despite the delicately lovely song, the call note is a harsh descending *veer!* The flight call is a strident, descending and then ascending *jhwuh-eet!*

The only thrush rusty above from head to tail, Veery also has the subtlest spots, which barely reach breast.

Gray-cheeked Thrush

Catharus minimus

L 7.25″ | **WS** 13″

This uncommon thrush, shy and skulking and seldom found here except in May and September, is much less common and less likely to come into the open than the similar Swainson's Thrush, but often joins other thrushes in fruit trees during fall migration. Unlike Swainson's, it's grayish brown, rather than olive, above. May have a subtle eye ring, but never has a buffy or creamy spot in front of the eye. The Gray-cheeked migrates through but nests far north of here, so we seldom hear it sing. The nocturnal flight call is a burry but squeaky *beeoh!*

Grayish brown above from head to tail. Subtle or no eye ring on entirely gray face, spotted breast.

Swainson's Thrush

Catharus ustulatus

L 7" | **WS** 11.75"

This common migrant throughout breeds in coniferous forest of the northeast. It closely resembles the Gray-cheeked except for its prominent buffy eye ring. The olive back color can be hard to distinguish from the grayer Gray-cheeked even when they're close together. When breeding, it's heard far more often than seen. During migration, it's more visible, often in or near fruit trees, hopping robin-like on moist ground, and sometimes visiting birdbaths. The song spirals up, like a Veery in reverse. The call note is a rich *whit!* or *pip!* The nocturnal flight call is a spring peeper-like *peep*.

Creamy eye ring, with cream extending to the bill.

Back may appear brown, olive, or gray.

Hermit Thrush

Catharus guttatus

L 6.25" | **WS** 10.5"

This common *Catharus* thrush, the only one with a rusty tail contrasting with a grayish back, appears earlier in spring, remains later in fall, and occasionally winters here. When it rummages through leaf litter, it slowly raises and then lowers its tail, often several times a minute. When it flies away, it can be confused only with the Fox Sparrow due to the rusty tail. Its haunting song starts with sweet notes at midrange and ends with high, thin notes. Gives a low *chuck* and a rising *scree?* that is less harsh than the Veery's *veer*. Its flight call is a clear, slightly descending *chee*.

Strongly spotted; rusty tail, subtle eye ring.

Often raises and lowers tail while foraging.

Wood Thrush

Hylocichla mustelina

L 7.75" | **WS** 13"

This uncommon and declining thrush breeds in hardwood forests, mostly in the southeast and rarely in the west. Larger, plumper, more brightly colored and boldly spotted than *Catharus* thrushes, it is heard more often than seen. The beautiful song is the most flute-like of all the thrushes, the first phrases rich and varied, the final notes high and thin, often transcribed as *ee-oh-lay*. The ending is similar to the Hermit Thrush's, the opening richer and deeper. The flight call is a harsh, low-pitched *cheat!*

Rich rusty head, back, and wings; clear eye ring. Deep black spotting extends to the belly.

American Robin

Turdus migratorius

L 9.5″ | **WS** 14″

This ostensible harbinger of spring winters wherever fruits are available. Tens of thousands can be counted in a day from Hawk Ridge and the North Shore during late September and early October. It flies directly, whipping the pointed wings back; from below or the side, the white undertail coverts are conspicuous. The territorial song, sweet and melodic, is a leisurely "sentence" composed of 2- and 3-syllable "words," frenetically hurried at dawn. Calls include a soft, fairly low *tuck*; a louder, sharper *peek* often followed by a few *tuck* calls; and a rapid-fire *kee-kee-kee-kee-kee*.

Juvenile's spotted breast usually shows some orange.

Dark head, white eye ring and throat streaks; yellow bill.

Varied Thrush

Ixoreus naevius

L 8.75″ | **WS** 14.25″

This "fancy robin" from the Pacific Northwest, very rare in fall and winter, is shy but conspicuous at backyard fruit trees or lurking on the ground below feeders, usually near a stand of conifers. One may remain in a yard for a week or more, or may vanish before you can grab the camera. Male's facial and breast markings are black, softer gray in females. Male has orange throat, eyebrow, wing markings, and belly; female's are duller. We seldom get to hear the eerie whistled song, but while one is here, it occasionally makes a low *chup* and harsher *churr* notes.

Black crown, facial markings, breast band, and back.

Female similar to male but more softly colored.

Gray Catbird

Dumetella carolinensis

L 8.5″ | **WS** 11″

This lithe skulker of dense underbrush and tangles, a common summer resident throughout, arrives in late April or May, and sometimes visits feeders for jelly or mealworms. Almost entirely gray with a black bill, crown, and tail; the dark eye stands out on the unmarked face. Rusty undertail coverts are distinctive but hard to see. The song, which can last 10 minutes, is a string of imitations of bird songs and various other sounds all jumbled together, sometimes punctuated with a catlike *mew*. The raspy *mew* call gives it its name; it also makes a variety of other calls, including a harsh *check!*

Gray, with black bill, crown, and tail. Dark eye, rusty undertail coverts. Slender and long.

Brown Thrasher

Toxostoma rufum

L 11.5" | **WS** 13"

This exuberant singer arrives in late March or April, weeks before catbirds but in similar dense habitat. It often scratches the ground, where it is sometimes mistaken for a thrush; the thrasher is streaked rather than spotted, with wing bars and a yellow eye. It usually skulks in dense vegetation, but sings from an exposed perch. The song is a long string of imitations of birds and an extraordinary variety of other sounds, most delivered in pairs—one thrasher made it into *Ripley's Believe It or Not* for singing 2,400 different songs. The most common call note sounds like a loud, smacking kiss.

Long and slender, with slightly downcurved bill, yellow eye, wing bars, and streaking from breast through belly.

Northern Mockingbird

Mimus polyglottos

L 10" | **WS** 14"

This rarity can turn up anywhere at any time, but seldom sings here; nesting has been recorded only five times. It often sits on fences and wires; the long tail and plain face eliminate the possibility of a shrike. While foraging on open ground, it often lifts its wings, flashing bold white wing patches. The song is a thrasher-like string of imitations, most delivered three or more times; mockingbirds desperate for a mate aggravate people by singing all night long, but we're not lucky or unlucky enough to experience that here. The call they most often give here is a harsh *chew*.

Long and slender, mostly soft gray. Tail is black with white outer tail feathers. White wing bars, yellow eye.

European Starling

Sturnus vulgaris

L 8.5" | **WS** 14"

This 1890 import to New York City was first reported here in 1931; it quickly became abundant everywhere but dense northern forest. Short tail and chunky body distinguish it from blackbirds. The starling and Cedar Waxwing have a similar shape in flight due to triangular wings and short tails, and both move in flocks. The Starling weighs twice as much, with a beefier body, zooming by with more power and speed. Large flocks fly in dense formation, shape-shifting before our eyes. Related to mynas, its songs include many jumbled imitations as well as rattles, whirrs, and whistles. In spring, it throws in spot-on imitations of Eastern Wood-Pewee and Eastern Meadowlark. Call notes are varied; many have a squeaky quality. Nighttime roosts in lighted urban areas can be extremely noisy.

Breeding adult's glossy feathers have an oily sheen; the bill is bright yellow with a pink base in females, blue in males.

Winter starling is spangled with white; the thin bill varies from dark to yellowish. Can look very plump.

Juvenile is flat brown during its first summer; identified by general shape and the parents it noisily follows.

Bohemian Waxwing

Bombycilla garrulus

L 6.25–7.5″ | **WS** 13″

Two waxwings occur here, both crested and sleek with a black mask and yellow-tipped tail; both may have waxy red tips on some wing feathers. Bohemian, the larger, appears virtually every winter along Lake Superior's north shore, in mountain ashes and on the ground in snowmelt puddles. It is irruptive, either frustratingly hard to find or abundant. Flocks may number in the dozens or hundreds; occasionally joins robins. Scan every waxwing in any winter flock in case both species are present. Bohemian has rough, low-pitched chattering call, with many dry trills.

Gray breast and belly, rusty highlights on face and undertail. Wing markings are fancy, with yellow highlights in adults.

Cedar Waxwing

Bombycilla cedrorum

L 6" | **WS** 10.25"

This common summer resident arrives en masse as apple blossoms open, often eating petals. A few winter, mostly in the south. Smaller than Bohemian, without chestnut on face or undertail. Gregarious; in mid-summer it gathers in large flocks to feed on fruit and flying insects and to migrate. Thousands can be counted from Hawk Ridge on late summer days. Flight is more leisurely than the similarly shaped starling, but counting is tricky because individuals shift positions, making the flock seem to swirl as it moves. Calls include very high-pitched lisps and trills, like tiny mice snoring.

Adult has brown breast, yellow belly, white under tail. Juvenile streaked, with black mask and yellow-tipped tail.

American Pipit

Anthus rubescens

L 6″ | **WS** 10.5″

A slender, drab migrant, uncommon in spring in the west; common in fall, mostly along shorelines, and rather common at Park Point in Duluth. Resembles a slender-billed, long-legged sparrow, and bobs its tail like a waterthrush or Palm Warbler. Buffy underparts and a necklace of delicate streaks on the breast, subtler in fall, are useful clues, and the white outer tail feathers are helpful in flight. It appears in the same fields as thicker-billed larks and longspurs, which don't bob the tail. Frequently gives a squeaky, goldfinch-like *pipit* or *slip-it* call, especially in flight.

Slender bill. Pale above bill and behind eye, streaky necklace across breast. White outer tail feathers best seen in flight.

Lapland Longspur

Calcarius lapponicus

L 6″ | **WS** 9–11″

This hardy sparrow-sized bird of the tundra is common in open country, mostly in the south and west, in March and April, and throughout in fall, when it can be easy to observe along Lake Superior and at Hawk Ridge. Our only longspur from November through March; gathers with Snow Buntings and Horned Larks in agricultural fields and along roadsides. Stout bill, short legs, brown cheek bordered below and behind with black, rusty shoulder, white outer tail feathers. Doesn't pump tail. Husky *zeep* call, chips, and rattles, frequently given in flight, are similar to Snow Bunting's.

Note black on face, white outer tail, unstreaked breast.

Feather wear in spring may reveal male's breeding pattern.

Chestnut-collared Longspur

Calcarius ornatus

L 5-6" | **WS** 11"

This is the only longspur present in the state from June through August, but you'll have to head to the Felton Prairie in Clay County to see it. Listed as Endangered, any sightings outside of its tiny breeding range must be carefully documented. Breeding male, the easiest to see, is beautiful and distinctive, perched or in flight. Female and non-breeding male much drabber. In flight, the white tail with black inner triangle is distinctive. Gives soft *cheer* or *quiddle* calls and a purring chatter; the song is a short, musical warble like a Western Meadowlark.

Thick bill, plain face. Underparts mottled, not streaked.

Male has chestnut nape, buffy throat, white triangle on tail.

Smith's Longspur

Calcarius pictus

L 6-7" | **WS** 11"

This extremely rare longspur is expected only in mid-October in western grasslands such as Rothsay Wildlife Management Area in Wilkin County or the Russell Sewage Ponds in Lyon County. Smith's appears before Lapland Longspur migration peaks, but both species can be present at the same time. In some years, a Minnesota Ornithologists' Union field trip is timed specifically to look for it. May also appear elsewhere in spring and fall, especially Duluth and north shore, but should be carefully documented. The rattle calls can be slower and longer than those of Lapland Longspur.

Uniformly buffy underparts with diffuse streaking. More slender bill and more white on tail than Lapland.

Snow Bunting

Plectrophenax nivalis

L 10″ | **WS** 11″

The plump "snowflake" is common during fall throughout; less common in winter and spring, mostly in the west. It shuffles along on short legs on fields and roadsides, often associating with slightly smaller Horned Lark and Lapland Longspur. In fall and winter, many feathers are edged with buffy cinnamon that starts wearing off by spring, revealing more black and white; stragglers in May can be very white, usually with some buff still evident. Large white wing patches are always conspicuous in flight. Frequently gives husky, rolling rattle calls and sharp *tidik!* calls, especially in flight.

Short legs; many feathers edged with cinnamon.

Stragglers in May show more black and white.

Ovenbird
Seiurus aurocapilla

L 6″ | **WS** 9.5″

This forest warbler, common from May through September throughout, especially the eastern half, is the subject of a Robert Frost poem for its persistent singing. Despite the ringing song, it can be tricky to locate, staying at mid-height and seldom moving during singing bouts. When not singing, it walks on the ground in a distinctive herky-jerky, seemingly random way. Often found dead under windows. The song, often described as *teacher, teacher teacher*, sounds more like *da CHEER, da CHEER, da CHEER, da CHEER*.

Snow-white with black spots beneath, olive brown above. White eye ring, pinkish bill and legs. Orange crown edged with black.

Louisiana Waterthrush

Parkesia motacilla

L 6″ | **WS** 10″

The two waterthrushes, which are not thrushes but warblers, are constant tail bobbers. This one, a species of Special Concern, breeds mostly along heavily wooded creeks in the southeastern quarter of the state, such as at Whitewater State Park and along the St. Croix River, where it's the only waterthrush in June and July. Where both occur in migration, note the shape of the eyebrow and any throat streaking. Louisiana never has buffy underparts. The loud, sweet song starts with 2–5 clear descending whistles, such as *dear, dear, dear; cheery, cheery.* The call is a sharp metallic *chip!*

Eyebrow, always white, extends to the nape; the throat is unstreaked, and the streaked underparts are whitish.

Northern Waterthrush

Parkesia noveboracensis

L 6″ | **WS** 9.5″

The only waterthrush found in northern swamps and bogs in summer, this is a fairly common migrant throughout in May and late August through September, when both species may occur in southeast. Underparts are usually more yellowish or cream-colored than Louisiana's. During fall migration it often appears in tangles far from water. Often remains hidden while singing its loud, ringing song, similar to the rarer Connecticut Warbler's, a choppy series of one-pitch phrases that ends with one or more *whew*-like notes: *So much to do, much to do. Finished this, Whew!* The call note is a loud, hard *spwik*.

Eyebrow, often cream rather than white, usually tapers before nape; streaked throat; streaked underparts often buffy.

Golden-winged Warbler

Vermivora chrysoptera

L 4.75" | **WS** 7.5"

This tiny warbler, declining over most of its range, is uncommon but widespread in brushy habitat with aspens in the northeastern two-thirds of the state; it's generally hard to find during migration. Often forages in high branches, where the black-bibbed male can be mistaken for a chickadee. Black is replaced by soft gray in female and juvenile. White underparts tinged with gray. Song starts with an extremely high-pitched buzz (inaudible to some) followed by three slightly lower-pitched buzzes: *Seee, bzz bzz bzz.* Can also sing the Blue-winged's song.

Adult male with striking head pattern.

Female and juvenile soft gray; yellow on head and wing patch.

Blue-winged Warbler

Vermivora cyanoptera

L 4.75″ | **WS** 7.5″

This tiny, bright treetop warbler, fairly common in the south-eastern third, is steadily extending its range north. It freely hybridizes with Golden-winged, which usually dwindles and disappears as Blue-winged spreads into its breeding range. Blue-wingeds with yellow-tinged wing bars may be hybrids. Blue-winged's wing bars and tapered eye line, as if wearing makeup, distinguish it from larger, bulkier Prothonotary. The most commonly heard song is a high buzz followed by a lower trill, sounding almost like it's blowing a raspberry, *Bee-pbbbbbhhht*. Can also sing Golden-winged's song.

Sexes similar. Lemon-yellow head and underparts, tapering eye line, bluish wings with wing bars. Large white tail spots.

Black-and-white Warbler

Mniotilta varia

L 5.25″ | **WS** 8.25″

This licorice-black and snow-white bird breeds in northern hardwood and mixed forests in the northeastern half, and is a common migrant throughout in May and September. Often seen creeping along tree trunks and large limbs, moving up, down, and around like a creeper or nuthatch. Our only black and white warbler with a white crown stripe; also has unique black chevrons beneath the tail, fairly conspicuous as it works its way around branches. The most commonly heard song is a squeaky *weesee weesee weesee weesee*. Blackburnian often sings a similar song, a bit higher and shorter.

Adult male with black mask, bib, and striped crown.

Female with soft gray cheek, black and white crown.

Prothonotary Warbler

Protonotaria citrea

L 5.5" | **WS** 7"

This stunning golden-yellow bird, our only cavity-nesting warbler, is an uncommon, local summer resident in wooded backwaters of rivers in the southeastern third of the state, and is seldom seen elsewhere during migration. Sightings become sporadic at best by August. Large and robust for a warbler, the sexes are similar, but males more intensely colored, with subtle orangey highlights. Broad, square tail is mostly white beneath, with a narrow black tip; shows large white patches from above. The song is a simple string of identical notes, *Sweet, sweet, sweet, sweet, sweet.*

Round dark eye on plain yellow face; thin, pointed bill. Bluish wings lack wing bars. Short square tail white beneath.

Tennessee Warbler

Leiothlypis peregrina

L 4.75″ | **WS** 7.75″

This common migrant throughout and local breeder in the
northeast is easier to identify by song than plumage. It's much
tinier and quicker than Red-eyed Vireo, with a tiny bill; the
gray crown is never edged with black. The similar Orange-
crowned Warbler passes through early in May, and is much
rarer in August and early September. In all plumages, the
Tennessee's undertail coverts are whiter than the breast, and
there is a broad eyebrow. The song, one of the longest warbler
songs, is loud and emphatic, with three distinct phrases, *dit dit
dit dit dit, cheat cheat cheat, titititititititi.*

In spring, gray head
contrasts with greenish
back, wings, and tail.

In fall, yellowish
below, with white
undertail coverts.

Orange-crowned Warbler

Leiothlypis celata

L 5″ | **WS** 7.5″

This tiny warbler is the "sort of" bird: it's sort of yellowish or olive, with sort of eye rings or eye crescents, sort of an eye line, and is sort of streaked below. Spring male has sort of an orange crown. Tennessee is most similar, but Orange-crowned has yellow undertail coverts and its face is more subtly marked; Tennessee never has even subtle streaking. Orange-crowned nests far north of here and is not seen in summer. Migration peaks in early May and in October. The song, not often heard in spring migration, is a wavering 1- or 2-part trill.

Very low-contrast plumage, dull yellowish or olive overall.

Even grayish birds have yellow undertail; eye ring subtly broken.

Nashville Warbler

Leiothlypis ruficapilla

L 4.25″ | **WS** 7.25″

This tiny warbler, common in northern forests from early May through October, migrates throughout, sometimes appearing at birdbaths. Active, but can stay concealed in conifer even when singing nearby. Adult male's rusty crown is usually hard to see even at close range. The larger Connecticut has a gray throat. Nashville's eye ring more complete than Orange-crowned's. Drab fall birds can have faint wing bars and more subtle eye ring. The song, quieter than the Tennessee's, is a 2-part *seeBIT, seeBIT, seeBIT, seeBIT, see; weet tweet tweet tweet tweet*.

Bold white eye ring on plain gray face, yellow throat and undertail.

Connecticut Warbler

Oporornis agilis

L 5.1–5.9″ | **WS** 8.6″

Birders from around the country come to the Sax-Zim Bog and other spruce tamarack bogs from late May to early July to see this uncommon large, skulking warbler. During migration it is possible anywhere. The bold white eye ring stands out on the evenly gray head and upper breast; the much smaller Nashville shares the eye ring, but has a yellow throat. The song is a loud and jerky *chuppity, chuppity, chuppity,* richer and less sweet than a Common Yellowthroat, and most often confused with the Northern Waterthrush's. The Connecticut doesn't end its song with a *whew!* note.

Solid gray hood extends to breast. Complete round eye ring, soft yellow underparts, large pinkish bill, pink legs.

Mourning Warbler

Geothlypis philadelphia

L 4-6" | **WS** 7"

This large, fairly common warbler of northern deciduous and mixed forests can stay hidden in the understory, skulking on big pink feet, but often sings from exposed perches. The male's dark gray hood, blacker between the eye and bill, ends in a jet-black smudge where it meets the breast. Female's hood can be softer gray like a Connecticut's, but Mourning never has a complete round eye ring. In fall, may have a bit of an eye ring and a pale throat rather than complete hood. The underparts are uniformly bright yellow. The most common song is a rich, burry *Cheese, cheese, cheese, for me, for me.*

Spring male has black lore and black smudge on breast.

Bigger, with a more massive bill than Nashville Warbler.

Common Yellowthroat

Geothlypis trichas

L 4.75″ | **WS** 6.75″

This abundant warbler breeds throughout the state in cattail marshes and brushy fields, where it acts wren-like, cocking its tail and chattering noisily at disturbances. Males have a black "bandit mask" with a wide whitish border above. Females lack the mask; their crown and face are brown, contrasting with the yellow throat, and they have a subtle eye ring. The back and wings are more brownish than olive. The song is a bright, cheerful *witchety, witchety, witchety, witchety*, or *Lookee here! Lookee here! Lookee here! Lookee here!* The call is a strong, cranky-sounding *chuck*.

Black mask edged with white. Brown above, yellow underparts.

Female mostly brown. Bright yellow throat, wren-like behavior.

Hooded Warbler
Setophaga citrina

L 5.25" | **WS** 7"

This species of Special Concern looks like a reverse yellow-throat, with a black hood and yellow mask. Female is brown-backed like female yellowthroat, but has white tail from beneath and a mostly yellow face. Both sexes flick and spread the long tail frequently to display white tail spots. Hooded breeds locally in hardwood forests in a small area centered between Afton and Lake Maria State Parks; birders search for it in late May and June. The short whistled song, richer than a Magnolia's, often ends with a descending note, *pee-chu, pee-chu, pee-chu-chu.* The call note is a thick *chip.*

Striking male with yellow underparts, white tail spots.

Female's yellow face contrasts with cap and back.

American Redstart

Setophaga ruticilla

L 5.25″ | **WS** 74.75″

Abundant from May through September in open woodlands, this lively and dainty sprite is easy to glimpse but hard to follow as it flits about anywhere from low shrubs to treetops. It switches and flares its tail and spreads its wings to show off orange or yellow patches; even in flight, the squarish yellow or orange tail patches identify it. Male takes over a year to attain adult plumage; year-old male can have black flecks in the gray plumage. Songs are short and sweet but extremely variable; the most recognizable versions end in an emphatic buzzy sneeze. The call note is a bright *chip!*

Adult male black, white, and orange.

Female gray and yellow; young male may have flecks of black.

Cape May Warbler

Setophaga tigrina

L 4.75" | **WS** 8.25"

This handsome tiger-striped warbler is an uncommon breeder in coniferous forests of the north and a common migrant in late spring and early fall. During cold snaps in May, some visit bird feeders for oranges, jelly, and sugar water. Male Cape May, Magnolia, and Canada Warblers all have heavily streaked yellow underparts; only Cape May's throat is streaked. Male's chestnut cheek patch bordered by eye line and bright yellow from throat to nape. Female's gray cheek patch bordered by softer yellow. The song is a very high-pitched, sweet, steady *seet-seet-seet-seet*.

Even, dense streaking on breast; wide white wing bar.

Even dullest female has yellow behind the cheek.

Cerulean Warbler

Setophaga cerulea

L 4.75" **WS** 7.75"

This tiny, rare, and elusive treetop warbler, designated Special Concern, breeds locally in deciduous forests in the southeastern quarter of the state and is seldom seen beyond there. Our only blue-backed warbler with a pure white throat, the male has a dark bluish band across the breast—often the only field mark we can manage to see from below. Female is a soft aquamarine above and creamy yellowish or whitish beneath. Both have wing bars, an eye line, and streaked sides. The song starts slow and ends on a higher buzzy trill: *cheat, cheat, cheat, busy busy zeet.*

Breast band and streaked sides visible from below.

Female soft aquamarine and yellowish or whitish.

Northern Parula

Setophaga americana

L 4.5" | **WS** 7"

Our tiniest warbler breeds in northern forests wherever *Usnea* lichens drape trees, and migrates throughout. It's very active and usually stays high in trees, but spends a lot of time in outer branches, making it easier to watch than other forest warblers. In June, scan clumps of *Usnea* and you may detect a nest, giving you a chance to watch the birds coming and going. From below, note adult male's yellow throat and breast, separated by a blue band and patch of chestnut; from above, note the yellowish green patch on the back. The song is a rising buzzy trill, often ending with a sharp hiccup.

Male's lower bill blends with throat. Pure white belly.

Even drab females have contrasting yellowish patch on back.

Magnolia Warbler

Setophaga magnolia

L 5″ | **WS** 7.5″

This licorice and lemon beauty breeds throughout northern coniferous forests and is a common migrant throughout. The spring male has striking face markings and a large white wing patch; his yellow breast is streaked with black, starting at a "necklace" below the bright yellow throat. Female and fall male much duller. In any plumage, unique white tail with a thick black tip, noticeable even when it flies overhead. When it flits about, often at eye-level, it flares the tail frequently as if to show off this feature. The song is short and sweet, a hurried *weo, weo, wee, ti-ti.*

Spring male has black face framed by eye crescent and eyebrow.

In fall, note eye ring and wing bars, delicate streaking.

Bay-breasted Warbler

Setophaga castanea

L 5.5" | **WS** 9"

This handsome warbler, which breeds locally in northern spruce forests, especially along the Gunflint Trail, is one of the harder "common" warblers to see here. Spring male unmistakable. Female and fall male can be mistaken for Blackpoll Warbler, with steaked greenish gray back, wing bars on gray wings, and a creamy or white eye ring and underparts. A hint of chestnut coloring on neck or sides can clinch an identification, or look at the leg color: Bay-breasted has black legs, the Blackpoll yellow. The song is very high and weak like the Cape May's, but the notes are more run together.

Breeding male with creamy nape and underparts, dark face.

Fall birds have unstreaked underparts, dark legs and feet.

Blackburnian Warbler

Setophaga fusca

L 5″ | **WS** 8.5″

Orange sherbet and licorice would not go together in any sensible diet, but their colors look splendid on this stunning and common beauty of northern mixed forests. It feeds and sings high in the canopy, but also frequents quiet streams and pools for drinking and bathing, and often appears at birdbaths during migration. The song is extremely high-pitched and variable. One common song sounds like the Black-and-white Warbler's, but shorter and higher-pitched: *wee-see, wee-see, wee-see*. Another starts with a short, sweet, high-pitched phrase and ends with an extremely high trill.

Spring male is orange, black, and white.

Female and immature face pattern similar to male's but more subtle.

Yellow Warbler
Setophaga petechia

L 5″ | **WS** 7″

This wetland warbler breeds near willows or other shoreline
trees. Male has chestnut breast streaks and darkish edging on
flight feathers. The wings are more patterned than a Prothonotary's, and the Yellow has no white under the tail. It's
conspicuous from May to early July, and then becomes hard
to find. The song is a distinctive *Sweet, sweet, sweet. Aren't I
sweet?* The alternate song is like a Chestnut-sided Warbler's
Pleased ta MEETCHA! but usually a bit shorter; habitat helps,
because Chestnut-sideds are found in drier upland habitats.
Yellows make several different chips, some loud.

Spring male is
yellow with chestnut
streaking, dark eye.

Female and fall male
are dull yellow, may
have subtle eye ring.

Chestnut-sided Warbler

Setophaga pensylvanica

L 5" | **WS** 7.75"

This easy-to-find warbler of open mixed forests in the north-eastern third, a common migrant throughout, is usually seen at about eye level. Always white from the throat through the entire center of the underparts, it has a yellow or greenish yellow crown. In spring, the chestnut sides are obvious; adult males retain at least some chestnut in fall. The most characteristic song is a loud *Pleased, pleased, pleased ta MEETCHA!* The Yellow Warbler's alternate song is similar, but Chestnut-sideds don't nest or sing in the marshy areas where Yellow Warblers do, though they may be in nearby uplands.

Spring male distinctive; often holds tail up, wings down.

In fall, always has greenish yellow crown and eye ring.

Blackpoll Warbler

Setophaga striata

L 5.5" | **WS** 9"

This long-distance traveler passes through quickly in spring and fall. Spring male has chickadee-like cap and cheek, but streaked back and sides, a white throat, and a shorter, wider tail. The crown is unstreaked, unlike Black-and-white Warbler. Fall male dramatically different, with a greenish gray streaked back, wing bars on gray wings, and a creamy or white eye ring and underparts. Blackpoll usually has yellow legs and feet and streaked sides. Blackpoll often sings on migration; the song is a series of identical short, ringing, extremely high-pitched notes: *tsit, tsit, tsit, tsit, tsit.*

Spring male like a stocky, streaked chickadee.

Note the streaked back and sides, wing bars, bright feet.

Black-throated Blue Warbler

Setophaga caerulescens

L 5.25" | **WS** 7.75"

This elegant warbler nests locally in maple-basswood forests of Lake and Cook Counties, especially in and near Tettagouche State Park; it migrates through in small numbers, mostly in the east. Male striking; female an odd shade of greenish with hints of steel blue, with subtle cheek patch and creamy curved eyebrow. The small "handkerchief," a white spot on the edge of the folded wing, is unique and helpful, but lacking in some first-year females. The song is a series of husky, buzzy notes, the last slurred upward: *I am so laaaZEEEE.*

Male unmistakable. Note the white "handkerchief."

Female with curved eyebrow, dark cheek; wing patch may be absent.

Palm Warbler

Setophaga palmarum

L 5.5″ | **WS** 8″

This abundant early spring and late fall migrant breeds locally
in open bogs of the north. Plumage is extremely variable;
chestnut crown and yellow throat and breast vary by season
and subspecies. No matter what it looks like, the tail-pumping
habit draws attention to bright yellow undertail coverts. Alone
or in loose flocks, it spends a lot of time on the ground, often
near water, and also frequents roofs, lawns, and parking lots;
when it flies up, it flashes white tail corners. The song is a
rolling, buzzy trill mostly sung on the nesting grounds. The call
note is a strong, rather liquid *tsk*.

In spring, chestnut
crown, yellow on
face and throat.

Some fall birds very
dull except for
yellow undertail.

Pine Warbler

Setophaga pinus

L 5.5" | **WS** 8.75"

This early spring migrant nests in pine forests in the northeastern third; in cold snaps during migration, it may visit suet feeders, but otherwise is rarely seen far from pines, where it stays hidden most of the time. Male is yellower than female; both have wing bars, unstreaked back, diffuse streaking on sides, and whitish undertail, but even brightest male seems fairly low-contrast. The song, like that of Chipping Sparrow, is a simple steady trill on one pitch. Pine's song often sounds a bit more musical than the Chipping's typical dry trill.

Yellow-throated Vireo larger, Blue-winged Warbler brighter.

Drabbest Pine still has wing bars, diffuse streaking on sides.

Yellow-rumped Warbler
Setophaga coronata

L 5″ | **WS** 8.25″

This most abundant warbler in the state is first to arrive in spring and last to leave in October or early November. It's a common breeding bird in northern forests, and one or two may even overwinter in the south. In recent years it's appeared in increasing numbers at suet feeders during migration, especially during cold snaps. Plumage is extremely variable. Spring male is striking: shiny black and white with brilliant yellow on crown, at bend of wings, and on rump. Female and immature are drabber, with little or no yellow except on the rump. Birds of all ages often droop their wings. The song is short and sweet, with a rolling quality, and often 2-parted: *see see see, fiddledeedee*. The distinctive call, a dry, disapproving *tcht!*, is given frequently.

Spring male is striking, with yellow on crown and sides of breast as well as rump. Looks very sleek on hot days; fluffs out on frigid mornings.

Females and fall birds can be extremely drab, but may show a hint of yellow on breast sides.

In any plumage, often cooperatively droops wings to show yellow rump.

Black-throated Green Warbler

Setophaga virens

L 5.25" | **WS** 7.75"

This warbler's pleasantly sleepy tones drift from the treetops in mixed forests of the northeast beginning in early May. A constant presence through September and a persistent singer through mid-July, it usually stays hidden in the upper story. All plumages share a yellow face, white wing bars, greenish crown and back, and white belly. The two song types are buzzy but musical, with a whispery quality: *zee, zee, zee, zee, zoo-zee!* and *zhree, zhree, zoo zoo zee.* Songs can be heard through open car windows even as we drive through the woods at the speed limit.

The black throat it's named for is found only on adult male.

Female and young are quiet; seen most often in migration.

Canada Warbler

Cardellina canadensis

L 4-6" | **WS** 6.75-8.75"

This active little warbler, which arrives late and leaves early, is uncommon in mature deciduous or mixed forests in the north-east, usually in shady deciduous undergrowth in wet areas. During migration it can appear just about anywhere. The black necklace streaks don't extend as far down the breast as on the Magnolia, which has a completely different face and wing pattern. The perfect eye rings and yellow-bordered lore give it an earnest but somewhat cross-eyed appearance when viewed head-on. The song is short and snappy, more sputtery than the Magnolia's; it usually starts with a low *chip*.

Round eye ring, black necklace, bright yellow underparts, unmarked dark bluish gray back. Female similar but lacks necklace.

Wilson's Warbler

Cardellina pusilla

L 4.25″ | **WS** 6″

This tiny, active migrant throughout is also a rare and local nester in Lake and Cook Counties. It's usually found in brushy tangles, especially willows, near water, often at or below eye level. The male's black skullcap is unique. Male and female are plain above and plain yellow below, with no white in the tail. The dark eye stands out on the yellow face. One song is a rapid, unmusical series of identical notes, not quite fast enough to be a trill: *queep, queep, queep, queep, queep*. Another song is a series of sweet, slurred, thin notes: *dear, dear, dear, dear*. Call is a husky *jip!*

Adult male's dark eye and black beanie distinctive.

Female and young greenish above, yellow face and underparts.

Yellow-breasted Chat
Icteria virens

L 7″ | **WS** 9.75″

This extremely rare spring migrant and summer visitor, mainly in
the west and south, looks like a Common Yellowthroat on steroids,
but many researchers believe it's not closely related to warblers
at all. It skulks in dense vegetation and can be hard to see, but its
song is loud and attention-grabbing, making discovery a bit more
likely. If you're tracking a hotline or eBird report, listening will be
extremely helpful. The very loud song incorporates whistles, mews,
rattles, gurgles, imitations, and other bizarre notes, most repeated
several times. Its call note is a distinctive raspy *zhoot!*

Note heavy bill and striking
face. Strong contrast
between olive back and
crown, white belly, and
yellow throat and breast.

Eastern Towhee

Pipilo erythrophthalmus

L 8.5″ | **WS** 10.5″

This oversized, fairly solitary sparrow spends most of its time in dense underbrush and on the ground, where it scratches vigorously for seeds and insects. It's fairly common but local during migration, and nests here and there in all but the northeastern corner. The Spotted Towhee of the western states, once thought to be the same species, is a very rare visitor; its back and wings are boldly spotted with white. The three-part song is often described as *Drink your tea!* The "drink" is a metallic, sharp note, the "tea" a rapid trill. The call is a softly buzzy, rising *zhuhreee*.

Male black, white, and deep rust. Red eyes.

Female similar to male, but brown instead of black.

American Tree Sparrow
Spizelloides arborea

L 5.5″ | **WS** 9.5″

This hardy sparrow is common in most of the state from October through April; local in the north in winter. It visits backyards, but is found in largest numbers in weedy fields and marshes, usually on the ground or in low vegetation. The red cap is similar to that of Chipping Sparrow; the rusty eye line on gray face is softer than the darker, narrower eye line of Chipping. The single central breast spot is also helpful. Male starts singing in late winter; the song is variable but always soft and very sweet, starting with clear notes followed by a jumble. The call note is a sweet *seet*.

Rusty cap and brown eye line contrast softly with gray face; soft brown sides. Usually a "tie tack" spot in center of breast.

Chipping Sparrow

Spizella passerina

L 5.25" | **WS** 8.25"

This handsome little sparrow, abundant from April through early October, arrives in spring while some American Tree Sparrows are still present. The Chipping is flatter-headed, with a white eyebrow contrasting with the black eye line; the throat is whiter, and the sides are gray rather than soft brown. The song is a long, steady, dry trill like someone rolling d's on the tongue. Even experts confuse some of its songs with other birds, though the Chipping Sparrow's is usually drier and more mechanical than the Pine Warbler's and longer and less musical than the junco's. The *chip* is short and dry.

Adult's eye line is black, underparts and sides whitish gray.

Juvenile, common in summer, is densely streaked, lacks red cap.

Clay-colored Sparrow

Spizella pallida

L 4.9-5.5″ | **WS** 7.8″

This petite, delicately beautiful sparrow is found from May
through September throughout, in open areas with scattered
shrubs, especially small conifers; it occasionally visits feeders
during spring migration. It's pink-billed, with white striping
on brown face and crown, and a contrasting soft gray nape.
Young birds are streaked like young Chipping Sparrows, and
can be hard to distinguish without a parent or other adult
nearby. Often sings from an exposed perch. The song is a dry,
simple, insect-like buzz repeated two or more times: *bzzz, bzzz,
bzzz, bzzz.*

Light gray nape contrasts
with brown cheek patch.
White eyebrow, crown
stripe, and throat. Long tail.

Field Sparrow

Spizella pusilla

L 5.75" | **WS** 8"

This tiny rusty and gray sparrow breeds in brushy fields in the southern two-thirds of the state; most leave by late October, but a straggler or two occasionally remain into December. The population is declining significantly. The pale, low-contrast facial markings give it a passive, sweet demeanor; the uniformly pink bill matches the legs and feet. The immature White-crowned Sparrow also has a rusty head and pinkish bill, but is much larger and flatter-headed, and absent from June through August. The unique and beautiful song is an accelerating series of clear, slurred whistles.

Head markings pale and softly defined, underparts suffused with soft rust. Compact build, with a long tail.

Vesper Sparrow

Pooecetes gramineus

L 5.75" | **WS** 9.5"

This large sparrow breeds in fields and grasslands throughout, most abundantly in the south and west; it's uncommon and local in the northeast. Streaked above and below but rather nondescript, it's designed to blend with the ground where it feeds. Its white outer tail feathers and a rusty patch at the bend of the wing, sometimes hidden, are useful field marks. The song is a bit like that of the Song Sparrow; both start with two or three identical notes and then break into a jumble of slurs and trills. The introductory notes of the Vesper are long and clear, more musical than a typical Song's.

Large, pale, streaky sparrow with a hint of an eye ring, a rusty shoulder patch, and white outer tail feathers.

Lark Sparrow

Chondestes grammacus

L 6-6.75" | **WS** 11"

This striking sparrow of farmlands and grassy habitats, designated a species of Special Concern, is uncommon and local but widespread in the west and south. Most reports in the state are concentrated from May through July, and it's apparently gone by October. Sociable, it's often seen in small flocks. Perched or feeding on a roadside, it's easily identified by its vivid face pattern and black breast spot. The long, rounded tail flares out when it flies up, flashing conspicuous white corners. The song is a leisurely but choppy jumble of trills, buzzes, clear musical whistles, and rattles.

Bold face pattern, clean white underparts with a small black "tie tack." White corners of the rounded tail visible in flight.

Savannah Sparrow

Passerculus sandwichensis

L 5″ | **WS** 8.25″

This unassuming sparrow of grasslands, weedy fields, and
pastures was once abundant from April into early November
throughout, though virtually never at feeders. Less common
now, it's still easy to find. Superficially it resembles the Song
Sparrow, but the dark breast streaks contrast more with the
white underparts. It has a smaller, pinkish bill, and usually a
yellow spot before the eye. The quiet song, easy to recognize
once you know it, is short and insect-like, with three parts: a
few quick hiccup notes, then a high buzz, and then a slightly
lower buzz: *tic-tic-tic, zeeeeee, zuh.*

Breast streaks
contrast strongly with
white underparts;
yellow lore and small
pink bill distinguish
from Song Sparrow.

Grasshopper Sparrow

Ammodramus savannarum

L 4.5″ | **WS** 8″

This secretive grassland sparrow, common in the west and more local in the southeast from spring through fall, is declining, but fairly easy to see at Afton State Park. Its head and bill seem oversized for its tiny body. The short tail, unstreaked pale breast, and large, innocent-looking eyes are all helpful features. The thin yellow line above the eye and yellow at the bend of the wing are the only splashes of bright color. Recordings can help you learn the insect-like songs of grassland sparrows before you strike out on the search. The Grasshopper's song is a short and simple *tic tic bzzzzzz*.

Sings from tall weeds, but a quick look at the flat, oversized head and bill may be all you see before it dives into the grass.

Henslow's Sparrow

Centronyx henslowii

L 4-5" | **WS** 8"

This elusive and endangered bird breeds very locally in weedy grasslands in the south and west. It is notoriously difficult to see and hear, even though it's a persistent singer at dawn and dusk. It stays near the ground except when singing from a weed stalk, which may not be any taller than surrounding plants. The face, more strongly patterned than the Grasshopper Sparrow's, has an olive wash. The song, a quick, thin hiccup, *tse-lick,* is insect-like and short; by the time you're even aware the bird is singing, the song is over.

Olive, finely patterned face; whitish stripes on dark back.

Upper breast is very finely streaked.

Le Conte's Sparrow

Ammospiza leconteii

L 5" | **WS** 7"

This elusive little bird with the steel-gray bill, described by Thomas Sadler Roberts as having a warm, old-gold suffusion like a twenty-dollar gold piece, is widespread and locally common in wet meadows and grassy bogs in the northern half of the state. It's extremely furtive, often running on the ground like a mouse rather than flushing, and often stays concealed in grassy vegetation even when singing. Crown stripe and chestnut streaks on nape distinguish from Nelson's. The song is a hissing buzz, starting and ending with one or more tiny *tic* notes. Singing usually limited to twilight and dark.

Orangey buff on head and unstreaked breast; gray cheek.

Striped back; narrow dark line behind eye widens at nape.

Nelson's Sparrow

Ammospiza nelsoni

L 5" | **WS** 7"

This uncommon and local species of Special Concern breeds in the same northwestern bogs and meadows as the elusive Yellow Rail, and both vocalize mostly at night. It's looked for most reliably at the McGregor Marsh in Aitkin County and Agassiz National Wildlife Refuge in early June. Nelson's resembles the much more common Le Conte's Sparrow, but the facial markings are darker and more defined, it lacks a central stripe on the dark crown, and the gray nape lacks chestnut streaks. The song is a weirdly echoing, hissing buzz as if gasping for breath, dropping in pitch at the end.

Orangey breast with diffuse streaking; eye line curves down.

Unstreaked crown; gray nape lacks chestnut streaks.

Fox Sparrow

Passerella iliaca

L 7″ | **WS** 10.25″

This oversized sparrow is a very common early spring and late fall migrant throughout and winters locally. It often scratches vigorously on the ground beneath backyard feeders. Clean gray areas on the head, nape, and back contrast beautifully with foxy red and white body feathers. Contrast of rusty rump and tail with the grayish lower back is conspicuous when it flies away. The rusty breast spots are blotchier than on smaller Song Sparrow. During a late snowstorm, the quiet song, combining sweet whistles and delicate buzzes, is as welcome as a spring breeze.

Gray on head and nape contrasts with overall rusty plumage.

Breast spots blotchy; often coalesce in central spot.

Song Sparrow

Melospiza melodia

L 5.75″ | **WS** 8.25″

Common and widespread from March through October, rare and local in winter in the southern half, this sparrow can be found in urban neighborhoods as well as brushy areas and edges of wilder habitat, often near water. It visits feeders and the ground below, especially in winter and colder periods during migration, but seldom scratches the ground. The highly variable song virtually always starts with two or three identical notes (not sweet and slurred like the Vesper Sparrow's) and then breaks into a jumble: *peace, peace, peace, all my little children peace.* The call note is a short *chirp.*

The head is strongly striped, sides and breast streaked. Note dark triangles on each side of the light throat.

Lincoln's Sparrow

Melospiza lincolnii

L 5.5″ | **WS** 7.75″

This sparrow, a bit smaller than the Song Sparrow, breeds locally in tamarack bogs in the north and migrates throughout; though fairly shy and secretive, it occasionally lurks near feeders. Streaking on the breast, head, and nape is very thin and delicate, as if painted with a fine brush. The delicately drawn gray and brown markings are suffused with creamy buff. It seldom sings during migration, but in northern bogs you can hear the warbling song; it starts with a few slurred, clear notes followed by a rich trill and high thin notes: *you, you, WEEEEE, sweet, aren't we?*

Very fine streaking on buff-washed breast; face softer gray with more delicate markings than Song Sparrow's.

Swamp Sparrow

Melospiza georgiana

L 5.75″ | **WS** 7.5″

This widespread sparrow of wetlands skulks in cattails and
shrubs; it's common throughout from April through October,
and winters locally in the south, but is easily found only in
spring and early summer, when it sings. The dark rufous cap,
wings, and tail contrast with the gray and buffy face, fairly
conspicuous white throat, and cold gray underparts. The
breast is a bit darker than the belly, often with subtle, diffuse
streaking; it sometimes has a small dark "tie tack" breast spot.
The most common song is a trill like a Chipping Sparrow at
half speed; the call is a loud, hard *chip*.

Darker overall than
most sparrows; white
throat can stand out.

May have "tie tack"
like the softer brown
American Tree Sparrow.

White-throated Sparrow

Zonotrichia albicollis

L 5.75″ | **WS** 9″

Colored and striped like an avian chipmunk, the White-throated Sparrow is abundant throughout the state in spring and fall, gathering in feeding flocks with other sparrows in the woods and in backyards. It breeds in northern forests; may remain locally in winter, especially near feeders, where it often scratches the ground, but not with the Fox Sparrow's vigor. Adult has clearly marked white throat, yellow lore, gray cheeks, paler gray underparts, and brown wings, back, and tail. Head is striped black and white or dark brown and tan. Subtle, diffuse streaks on breast are most distinct in fall. The clear whistled spring song has the rhythm *Old Sam Peabody, Peabody, Peabody*; in fall, some sing a pathetically short, tuneless version.

Half of all adult males and females have black and white head stripes and a bright yellow lore; both sexes sing.

Half of all adult males and females have drabber tan head stripes; these birds are less assertive.

In fall, underparts can be fairly heavily streaked.

Harris's Sparrow

Zonotrichia querula

L 6.5–8″ | **WS** 10.5″

This oversized sparrow with a conspicuous pink bill is an uncommon migrant in spring and fall, overwintering in small numbers locally, especially near feeding stations. Spring adult is striking, black from crown to throat, with contrasting gray cheeks. Fall bird is much more variable, but always browner on face and back, with varying amounts of black and brown on crown, throat, and breast. It stands with an upright, dignified posture. Song is a mournful series of minor-key phrases of three identical whistled notes, each phrase in a different key: *I'm so sad. I'm so sad. I'm still sad.*

In spring, grayish overall, with black face, gray cheeks and nape.

In fall, browner, with variable brown and black crown and breast.

White-crowned Sparrow

Zonotrichia leucophrys

L 6" | **WS** 9.5"

This chunky sparrow is a common spring and fall migrant
throughout; winters locally, usually near feeders. It flocks with
juncos and other sparrows, often venturing farther onto lawns
than its flock mates. It has a less flat-crowned, bull-necked profile
than the White-throated; it never has yellow lores, and the throat
is gray like the breast. Immature, with pink bill and rusty cap, can
be confused with the much tinier Field Sparrow. We hear the song
only in May. It starts with a few clear whistles like a White-throated's and continues with variable buzzes and trills.

Adult with flat head,
crown stripes, gray
throat and nape.

Immature's crown is
rusty brown, paler in
center; gray nape.

Dark-eyed Junco

Junco hyemalis

L 6″ | **WS** 8.5″

When our snowbird spreads its tiny wings and flies away, it shows white outer tail feathers. An abundant migrant throughout, it lingers through winter in smaller numbers, especially near feeders, and breeds in some northern forests. Extremely variable plumage, but adults share the pink bill, snow-white belly and undertail, and unstreaked upperparts. In the most common form here, the adult male is entirely slate-gray except for the white belly and undertail; female and younger male may have slightly paler edges to wing feathers and varying amounts of brown on back and sides. Recent fledglings are streaked below. Singing begins in late winter, usually before Chipping Sparrow returns; the song is a musical trill, usually shorter and more rolling than a Chipping's.

Adult males uniformly slate gray above with a white belly, white outer tail feathers, and a pink bill.

Females and younger birds variable; soft shades of gray and brown, with white belly and pink bill.

The gray sides and breast of some young birds may obscure edges of white belly.

Scarlet Tanager

Piranga olivacea

L 7″ | **WS** 11.5″

This fairly common summer resident of mature deciduous forests rarely appears at backyard suet feeders during cold snaps in mid-May; once it reaches its nesting territory, it stays frustratingly out of sight. Spring male is unmistakable, vivid scarlet and shining black, but in mid-summer, after breeding, he molts into drab yellow like the female and young; his wings remain darker than theirs. After leaving the breeding territory, adult and young are drawn to cherry and other fruit trees, where they feed quietly; from mid-July through September, one or more may be present, unobserved, in even an astute birder's backyard. The song is a hurried series of short burry phrases, often likened to a robin with a sore throat. The *chick-burr* call given by both sexes can be heard on migration, too.

Breeding male is shiny red with jet-black wings and tail.

Beginning in mid-July, male is a strange patchwork of yellow and red as he molts into female-like plumage.

Plain wings of female and young are darker than the olive back.

Summer Tanager

Piranga rubra

L 6.75″ │ **WS** 12.2″

This extremely rare visitor wanders here occasionally from much farther south; it's usually seen at a feeding station or backyard fruit trees, and often remains for days or weeks for birders to see. Any sighting should be carefully documented. Adult male maintains "summer" color year-round; female and young male are orangey yellow. The bill is proportionally longer than that of other tanagers; the wings are never black, and are always lighter than the wings of Scarlet Tanagers. Seldom sings its slightly burry, robin-like song here, but does give its quick clicking *pit-ti-tuck* call.

Adult male is solid red with a long bill; face is plain.

Wings of female and young are not much darker than back.

Western Tanager

Piranga ludoviciana

L 6.5–7.75" | **WS** 11.4"

This extremely rare visitor from western states, the only tanager with wing bars, turns up here and there at feeders, often in May. The blush of red on the adult male's face ends softly at the neck, unlike the patchy red and yellow of a molting male Scarlet Tanager, and yellow wing bars on black wings confirm the identification. The yellowish female has a gray back (olive in Scarlet Tanager) and wing bars. The burry song sounds like a Scarlet's. The soft, quick call note, a rising *piddleit*, sounds a bit like a Summer Tanager's call.

Stunning spring male has wing bars and a sturdy tanager bill.

Wing bars and gray back distinguish it from Scarlet Tanager.

Rose-breasted Grosbeak

Pheucticus ludovicianus

L 8″ | **WS** 12.5″

This eye-catching bird, common throughout from May through September, is most easily observed at feeders during migration. In the open deciduous forests where it nests, it usually stays hidden in foliage, but calls frequently. Female looks like a gigantic female Purple Finch with white wing bars and an oversized bill; her wing linings, visible in flight, are yellow. In fall, young male, with buffy orange breast, can be mistaken for an extremely unlikely female Black-headed Grosbeak; in flight, the male Rose-breasted shows pinkish rather than yellow wing linings. The song, sung by both males and females, even on the nest, is a long, sweet, robin-like tune with a throatier, richer tone. The call, a sharp squeaky *chink!* often draws attention to one lurking in the foliage.

Adult male in breeding plumage is unmistakable; the oversized bill is pearly white.

Female has a strong facial pattern like female Purple Finch, but has wing bars and proportionally much larger bill.

Juvenile male's breast streaking varies. His underwing is pinkish.

Northern Cardinal

Cardinalis cardinalis

L 8.75″ | **WS** 12″

This striking bird, nonexistent in the state before the late
1800s, feeds on weed seeds, hides in brushy tangles, and avoids
mature forests and prairies. It's most abundant in the east-
central area radiating from the Twin Cities, still uncommon
in the west, and rare in the north outside of Duluth, where it's
now a fairly common permanent resident. Juvenile looks like
a scruffy, dark-billed female. The song, usually two-parted,
includes various rich whistled phrases such as *whoit, whoit,
whoit; cheer, cheer, cheer; pitchew, pitchew, pitchew,* and
tititititi. The call is a loud, hard *tik!*

Both sexes are
crested and
long-tailed, with a
thick red bill.

Female's mask small. Red highlights
on crest, wings, and tail.

Dickcissel

Spiza americana

L 5.5–6.2" | **WS** 9.8"

This irruptive bird of prairies and fallow fields is seen here mostly between June and August. It breeds mostly in the south but occasionally in the north, and rarely appears at feeding stations. Breeding male often sits on fences or wires; the pattern of his black breast band and the yellow on his face and breast superficially resemble a meadowlark's. His chestnut shoulder is distinctive. Female similar to female House Sparrow; the two species sometimes flock together during Dickcissel migration. The song is a simple, dry *dick dick dick cissel, trip.* The flight call sounds like a cranky *zhip!*

Far less streaked than meadowlark, bill shorter and stouter.

Note yellowish wash and thin line on side of female's throat.

Blue Grosbeak

Passerina caerulea

L 5.9–6.2" | **WS** 11"

This gorgeous bird has an extensive range, but barely makes it into Minnesota except in the extreme southwest. The much more common and widespread Indigo Bunting may be mistaken for this species; note the Blue Grosbeak's chestnut wing bars and larger, stouter bill. Female drab, but chestnut on upper wing bar and any bluish on rump and tail distinguish her from female cowbird. Reports from anywhere outside the southwestern corner of the state merit careful documentation. The male's rich, musical warble lasts 2–3 seconds. The call is a somewhat metallic *tick!*

Male has tiny black mask around the large bill, chestnut wing patches.

Female has chestnut wing bar; bluish tinge is variable.

Indigo Bunting

Passerina cyanea

L 5.5" **WS** 8"

This electric-blue bird is common and widespread but declining; it arrives in May, and may appear at bird feeders during migration. Male usually sings from power lines and snags, but often goes unnoticed because the stunning color can disappear in poor light. Female is plain brown, with a hint of diffuse streaking and subtle blue tinge in the tail. Indigos sing later into summer than most birds, not quieting down until August. Any finch with bluish seen in winter must be carefully documented. The buzzy, cheerful song is composed of short, mostly paired phrases that go on and on: *What? What? Where! Where! Got it! Got it! More? More?* The call note is a quick and thin *spit*.

Breeding male blue with blue wing bars, pale bill.

Female and fall male soft brown, with variable subtle blue wash.

Bobolink

Dolichonyx oryzivorus

L 7″ | **WS** 11.5″

This vulnerable grassland species breeds throughout except in the forested northeast, but is steadily declining; early mowing destroys nests. Breeding male is solid black from the crown through the underparts, largely white on the shoulders and lower back. His nape is dull yellow. Female and late summer male look like a Le Conte's Sparrow but larger, with an unstreaked nape; the two species often breed in the same fields. The song, often given as the male flutters low over the grasses, is an exuberant, bubbly, metallic jumble of squeaks and buzzes like R2D2. The call note is a sharp *pink*.

Breeding male with straw-colored back of head and nape, large white patches on wings and back. Stout black bill.

Female and non-breeding male the size of a large sparrow.

Red-winged Blackbird

Agelaius phoeniceus

L 8″ | **WS** 14″

Males appear in early spring, waging territorial skirmishes in cattail marshes in the morning, feeding in fields at midday; weeks later, when females arrive, males spend all day in breeding marshes. This abundant species breeds in wetlands and some brushy habitat throughout, and winters in large flocks south and west. Adult male's red epaulets are edged with a creamy stripe. Female plumage somewhat sparrow-like. Young male looks like female with rusty shoulders; second-year male is not yet solid black. In addition to the male's exuberant *okalee!* song, a huge variety of whistles and chips.

Non-displaying male hides epaulets, showing only the buffy edge stripe.

Female may have a bit of red on the shoulder or throat.

Eastern Meadowlark
Sturnella magna

L 9.5″ │ **WS** 14″

Our two species of meadowlark, present from early spring through late fall, often perch in the open on fences and wires. The chunky, short-tailed body, small head, and long bill give both a distinctive silhouette. The bright yellow underparts with large black breast band are striking, and the white outer tail feathers show conspicuously when they fan the tail in flight. The Eastern Meadowlark's song is a simple, sweet whistled *What cheer, spring is here!* It often gives a hard, dry rattle.

Breeding adult's yellow throat narrow, bordered by creamy or white malar stripes.

Western Meadowlark
Sturnella neglecta

L 8.25″ │ **WS** 16″

The Western Meadowlark is more common than Eastern in the west and south. Its rich, bubbly song is impossible for a mere human to imitate; its rattle is a bit lower than Eastern's.

Breeding adult's yellow throat appears wider than on Eastern.

Yellow-headed Blackbird

Xanthocephalus xanthocephalus

L 9.25" | **WS** 17"

This aptly named bird arrives in spring a bit later than Red-winged Blackbirds, and breeds in many of the same marshes as Red-wingeds, often in areas of deeper water. Most common in the west, it breeds in at least small numbers throughout the state except for the northeast, and joins large blackbird flocks in the south and west during migration. In flight, the male's large white wing patches are distinctive. The breeding song is a bizarrely comical production, starting with some musical notes and then breaking into a weird screeching buzz. It produces a dry *check* call year-round.

Black between eye and bill gives adult male a severe expression.

Adult female is brown, lacks white on wing. Juvenile much paler.

Rusty Blackbird

Euphagus carolinus

L 9″ | **WS** 14″

This dangerously declining species migrates through mostly in early spring and late fall, and winters in small numbers. In fall and winter, male has distinctive rusty feather edgings. Spring male differs only subtly from Brewer's Blackbird. Female Rusties have yellow eyes at all seasons. Rusty is usually found in wet, swampy habitat. It rarely visits feeding stations, Brewer's virtually never. The song sounds like a rusty hinge; the call note is a harsh *chek*.

Spring male smaller, less glossy, more delicate-billed, and much shorter-tailed than a grackle; less iridescent than Brewer's Blackbird.

Fall and winter Rusty has rusty-edged feathers, wide eyebrow.

Brewer's Blackbird

Euphagus cyanocephalus

L 8–10″ | **WS** 14.5″

This slender blackbird of short grasslands and agricultural areas is fairly common from March through October, and never here in winter; the similar Rusty occasionally winters, but is never present in summer. The iridescent purple head and pale eye give the breeding male Brewer's the look of a dainty, short-tailed grackle. The female is drab and unstreaked, rather like a female cowbird but more slender and a bit darker, with a thinner bill and longer tail. Female almost always has a dark eye, unlike female Rusty. The song is a squeaky, high-pitched *squeee!* It gives a variety of *tchup* calls.

Breeding male has purplish sheen on head; bill slightly thicker than Rusty Blackbird's.

Female usually darker than female cowbird; dark eye distinguishes from Rusty.

Common Grackle

Quiscalus quiscula

L 12.5″ | **WS** 17″

This grackle, abundant from early spring through October, remains in winter in smaller numbers, mainly in the south and west. Male arrives in March and immediately starts noisily displaying. When female appears a week or two later, they start nesting, usually in a conifer near water or in a residential area, but sometimes in a bird box or the lower sticks of an Osprey nest. By mid-June, noisy brown fledglings seem to be everywhere; by July, families form large flocks and retreat to more secluded areas to molt. Adult's iridescent head can have purple, green, or bronze highlights. Female is a bit smaller and less shiny than male. Calls include a wide variety of squeaks, whistles, croaks, and chips, some similar to those of Rusty and Brewer's Blackbirds.

Large, slightly curved bill and glittering eye give it a harsh look. Juvenile is brown with a dark eye through summer.

Great-tailed Grackle

Quiscalus mexicanus

L 15–18″ | **WS** 22.8″

This bird of Texas has spread northward and now breeds, rarely and locally, in the southwestern corner. The male is huge compared to the Common Grackle. His tail looks more outsized, and his purple iridescence seems more glowing. The female looks like a different species; she's brown and much smaller than the male—her own male fledglings look ridiculous begging from their relatively tiny mother. Forages on the ground in open areas, often in flocks. The calls are varied, including sweet tinkly notes, irritating squeals loud enough to be heard at a long distance, and all manner of mechanical sounds.

Adult male can fold his tail, as long as his body, into a distinctive keel shape.

Female is rich brown with blackish back, wings, and tail.

Brown-headed Cowbird

Molothrus ater

L 8″ | **WS** 14″

This small, chunky blackbird with a stout, finch-like bill arrives in large numbers in late March and April. Male calls, puffs out his feathers, and bows with opened wings in noisy displays. The all-gray female is quieter and more subdued, perhaps to avoid calling attention to herself as she lays her eggs in the nests of other birds. Juvenile is streaked below and more scaly-backed than the female; when first fledged, it follows its adoptive parent, usually a smaller species such as a warbler or sparrow, begging for food. By late summer, it joins with other cowbirds and molts into adult plumage. In addition to liquid gurgling display calls, cowbirds give a variety of squeaks and chattering calls.

Adult male has a stout black bill; the head is brown, and the body fairly shiny black.

Adult female is a flat, unmarked brownish gray with a thick black bill.

Juvenile of both sexes looks like female but is more streaked.

Orchard Oriole

Icterus spurius

L 7.25″ | **WS** 9.5″

This small oriole of open woodlands and river edges, present in the south and west from May through August, is less common and much more restricted in range than the Baltimore Oriole. It catches insects in the tops of trees, eats fruit and berries, and sometimes visits feeding stations for sugar water, orange slices, and jelly. Adult male's color is unique. Female is bright yellow and delicately proportioned; she is easily mistaken at first glance for a warbler. Her bill is more slender and pointed than a Scarlet Tanager's, which always lacks wing bars. The year-old male is yellow with a black face and throat. Paired male and female often seen together, but overall more solitary than Baltimore. The rich, melodious song is like a cross between a Purple Finch and a robin.

Adult male is black and brick red with virtually no white.

Female is patterned like the much tinier Blue-winged Warbler, but her bill is stouter.

It takes two years for a male to get the brick-red plumage. Until then, he's yellow with a black face and throat.

Baltimore Oriole

Icterus galbula

L 8.75″ | **WS** 11.5″

This brilliant blackbird is common and widespread throughout, from May through fall. It breeds in open deciduous woodlands, usually building its nest in a large shade tree near water. After nesting, it quietly retreats to fruiting trees, vines, and shrubs, often feeding in same trees as Scarlet Tanager. Adult male's orange plumage is unmistakable. Adult female is mostly yellow, with splotches of dark brown on head, throat, and nape. Juveniles are paler without the dark areas. The melody of the rich, clear, whistled song varies. The female also sings a short song. Both sexes give a harsh, dry rattle call.

Orange on tail and rump conspicuous when male flies away.

Adult female with dark brown on head, throat, and nape; less or no brown in juveniles.

Pine Grosbeak

Pinicola enucleator

L 8-10" | **WS** 13"

This large pink finch is an irruptive winter visitor in the north, much more common and widespread some years than others. It visits feeders, takes grit and salt from roadsides, and devours mountain ash, crabapples, and other fruit, sometimes with robins or waxwings. The head seems rather small on its plump body. The blackish bill is thick but not as oversized as in other grosbeaks. The large dark eyes have a gentle look. Female and young male can be yellow or russet. All plumages have pronounced wing bars on dark wings. It rarely sings here; its calls are mellow and warbling.

Adult male is pinkish red with soft gray on sides and lower belly.

Female and young male have yellowish or russet head, nape, and rump.

House Finch

Haemorhous mexicanus

L 5.25″ | **WS** 8.75″

Introduced into the eastern U.S. from the desert southwest in the 1940s, the House Finch reached Minnesota in the 1980s and is now a common permanent resident except in deep coniferous forest. The male's head, face, and upper breast are red or, rarely, orange; the color sometimes extends to his belly. The back and wings are always drab grayish. The female's face is plain, lacking Purple Finch's bold pattern. The song is a bubbly warble with some slightly raspy notes, often ending on an upslur. The call note is a rich but slightly buzzy *zhree* or *zherp*.

Male's wings and back are gray.

Female has a much plainer face than Purple Finch.

Purple Finch

Haemorhous purpureus

L 5.5" | **WS** 9.5"

More wine- or raspberry-colored than purple, the Purple Finch breeds in northern forests; its winter range and numbers vary enormously from year to year. The male's bright colors always extend to his lower belly and seem to seep into his back and wings as well, unlike the grayer House Finch. The female's cheek patch is bordered with white above and below. Both species visit backyard feeders, but the Purple Finch nests in wilder places. The song is a rich, bubbly warble with one or two low *zhrrr* notes thrown in, without a noticeable upslur at the end. The call note is a short, sharp, high *tink!*

The male's red color seeps into wings and back.

Female's face pattern like much larger female Rose-breasted Grosbeak's.

Red Crossbill

Loxia curvirostra

L 6.75" | **WS** 10.25"

This irruptive migrant and unpredictable breeder is found mostly in pine stands in the north. Deep red or dull yellow, it has an oversized bill with crossed tips. It feeds in the tops of large cone-bearing pines, but also picks up grit and salt along wintertime roads. Juvenile, which can appear as early as January, is brown and streaked; it may have narrow wing bars, but seldom strays far from its parents. Calls vary by subspecies, but all sound pretty much like *kip kip*. The song is also variable, with hard, short notes interspersed with richer phrases, *tick tick tick chuppity chuppity tick tick*.

Large-headed, short-tailed; dark wings with no wing bar.

Female is dull yellow or olive, with brighter rump and breast.

White-winged Crossbill

Loxia leucoptera

L 6–7″ | **WS** 10″

This irruptive migrant and rare breeder feeds on tamarack and spruce cones, which are more loosely attached than pine cones; when a flock feeds, some individuals are usually on the ground working on fallen cones. Like Red Crossbill, it also picks up grit on roadsides. Male is pink in winter, redder in spring; female is yellow and rather streaked. Wing bars are bold. Juvenile is heavily streaked, but also has wing bars. The call is a quick, short series of *chut chut chut* notes, weaker than the *kip kip* of the Red Crossbill. The song is a series of short trills, some dry or raspy, some more musical.

Prominent white wing bars on pink or red male.

Yellowish female indistinctly streaked.

Common Redpoll

Acanthis flammea

L 4.75–5.5" | **WS** 7.5–8.75"

This irruptive winter visitor from the far north, which appears most regularly in the northern two-thirds, is astonishingly hardy. In a big redpoll year, hundreds can crowd into a single feeding station, often joining other finches, especially plain-faced, dark-billed Pine Siskins. The redpoll has a red forehead, black lore and chin, and short yellow bill. Away from feeders, it gathers in large flocks in weedy fields and birch stands, and on roadsides for grit. The rising, canary-like *cheeeeee?* calls and a variety of cheerful *chip-chip-chippy-chip* calls lend a festive air to a winter day.

Adult male's breast suffused with red or pink.

Female can be icy gray or warm buffy.

Hoary Redpoll
Acanthis hornemanni

L 5-6″ | **WS** 9″

One or two of these extremely rare winter visitors can sometimes be picked out in a flock of Common Redpolls. The easiest
to identify are extremely pale and "frosty," their yellow bill
even shorter and a bit thicker than the Common's, as if they'd
been punched in the nose. But variation in redpoll populations
confuses even experts. The best way to clinch an identification
is to see the unstreaked rump, a feat made a bit easier because
the Hoary has the courteous habit of occasionally lowering its
wings. Its calls are similar to the chattering calls and rising
notes of Commons.

Male has a very faint
suffusion of pink on
the upper breast.

Often lowers
wings to reveal
unstreaked rump.

Pine Siskin

Spinus pinus

L 5" | **WS** 9"

This little finch breeds mostly north, and stages occasional winter irruptions throughout, often with redpolls. The siskin is much streakier than the redpoll, without a trace of pink or red. The relatively long, thin bill is never yellow, and the face has no black markings near the eyes or chin. The amount of yellow varies, but usually has bright yellow in the wing, most noticeable in flight. Siskins are extremely vocal, chattering and giving lots of canary-like *cheee?* calls. One of the most common and characteristic calls is a rising, zippy buzz: *zhreeeeee!*

Heavily streaked with a plain face; bill long and slender for a finch.

Some individuals show little or no yellow.

American Goldfinch
Spinus tristis

L 4.5-5" | **WS** 7.5-8.75"

Before 1961, the goldfinch was widely considered the state bird of
Minnesota. It breeds throughout and winters in varying numbers,
mostly in the southern two thirds. In late winter and late summer,
male is patchy as he molts his body feathers. The goldfinch selects
a mate in spring but doesn't nest until mid-summer, when thistle
and other weeds provide downy seeds for food and nesting materials. The song is a long series of twitters and warbles. The *potato
chip!* call, given in flight, draws our eyes to the bouncy flight. It
also occasionally gives a rising, canary-like *beeeeee?* call.

Spring male
stunning yellow,
black, and white.

Variable amounts
of brownish and
yellow in winter;
always unstreaked.

Evening Grosbeak

Coccothraustes vespertinus

L 6.5-7" | **WS** 12-14"

This increasingly rare winter visitor shows up regularly but unpredictably in the north, and small flocks are fairly reliable in the Sax-Zim Bog. Family groups appear, seemingly randomly, in summer. Most of the year, the adult's oversized beak is dull and chalky, but it turns grass-green in late winter when pairs start courting, and remains bright until the young are independent in mid-summer. Male of any age has one large wing patch; female has three smaller patches, suffused with yellow in juvenile. It's rare to see a lone Evening Grosbeak; this gregarious bird is seldom seen or heard outside of a flock. Not particularly territorial, the sounds it makes in courtship and near the nest are the same high-pitched notes and friendly, burry chirps it makes the rest of the time.

Yellow, black, and white adult male has a dark brown head with a yellow forehead and curled eyebrow.

Adult female is soft gray with a yellow wash on the nape and three white patches on the black wings.

Juvenile female lacks yellow nape patch; white wing patches are suffused with pale yellow. The bill is dark.

House Sparrow
Passer domesticus

L 6.25″ | **WS** 9.5″

Introduced from Europe, the House Sparrow first arrived in the state in 1876; it's now a permanent resident of towns, cities, and farmland everywhere but in dense forests. It's chunkier, with a thicker neck and breast and shorter tail, than most native sparrows. The male is handsome and colorful, his gray crown and cheek separated by a bright chestnut eye line wrapping around the nape. The female is much drabber, similar to the much rarer Dickcissels that may be found on the same fields in summer, but she lacks yellow on the breast. The *cheep cheep cheep* song and chattering calls are iconic sounds of cities and farms.

Male's cheek patch contrasts with bib and eye stripe.

Female's markings are muted; she has a buffy eye line.

Author Acknowledgements

How can I possibly acknowledge all the people who gave me so very much, bringing me to a point where Scott & Nix, Inc. would ask me to write a field guide?

My grandpa let me stand on his dining room chair so I could talk to his canaries eye to eye. My fifth-grade teacher, Arthur Borkowski, gave me a sense of validation—that my love for even lowly earthworms wasn't laughable. Bob Hinkle sparked my interest in nature in his environmental education course at Michigan State University in 1974.

That same year, my husband Russ asked his parents to give me my first field guide and binoculars for Christmas. He has always accepted with grace and equanimity my sudden and all-consuming obsession.

William L. Thompson and Donald Beaver, my two ornithology professors at Michigan State, grounded that passion in science. When the American Ornithologists' Union met in Madison, Wisconsin, in 1978, I met the man who would become my lifetime hero and role model, Chandler Robbins. He sets the gold standard for generosity of spirit toward human beings even as he tirelessly works to protect birds and the world we share with them.

Joan Brigham of the Fenner Arboretum cheered me on while my lifelist was still in single and double digits. I worked my way through college as a bank teller, injecting bird information into basic transactions; many of my customers started standing in my line to get their questions answered. Those customers and my elementary and junior high science students at St. James and Immaculate Heart of Mary Schools in Madison inspired my lifetime focus on the non-birding community.

In 1979, Peter Fox asked me to write an article about warblers for the *Wisconsin State Journal*, and then kept asking for bird articles, setting in motion my entire writing career. Ken Wood, my shy friend and constant birding companion in Madison, helped me overcome my own shyness to lead field trips and get comfortable talking to birding groups.

When we moved to Duluth in 1981, three little babies did their best to distract me from birding, but as they turned into toddlers, children, and now adults, Joe, Katherine, and Tom accepted and even took pride in my birding pursuits. They helped me when I was rehabbing birds during their childhood, went along with a minimum of complaining when I dragged them to sewage ponds, and provided voices now and then for my radio show. Katherine recently created a database and website that make 30 years of radio programs and all my photography easily available for everyone at lauraerickson.com. I gave my children their first field guides long ago. This one is dedicated to them.

—Laura Erickson
Duluth, Minnesota

Scott & Nix Acknowledgments

Many thanks to Laura Erickson, and to Jeffrey A. Gordon, Louis Morrell, and everyone at the American Birding Association for their good work.

Special thanks to Curt Matthews and Joe Matthews at Independent Book Publishers (IPG).

Thanks to Alan Poole, Miyoko Chu, and especially Kevin J. McGowan at the Cornell Lab of Ornithology for their bird measurement data sets.

We give special thanks to Brian E. Small for his extraordinary photography and to all the others whose images illuminate this guide, including Alan Murphy, Bob Steele, Jim Zipp, Joe Furman, Laura Erickson, Mike Danzenbaker, Reinhard Geisler, and the photographers represented by VIREO (Visual Resources for Ornithology).

We thank Rick Wright, Harry Kidd, and Paul Pianin for their excellent work on the manuscript and galleys; Ann Antoshak Gallagher and Vicki Scott for layout; James Montalbano of Terminal Design for his typefaces; Charles Nix for design; and René Nedelkoff and Nancy Wakeland of Porter Print Group for shepherding this book through print production.

Image Credits

(T) = Top, (B) = Bottom, (L) = Left, (R) = Right; pages with multiple images from one source are indicated by a single credit.

XIII–XIV Brian E. Small. XIX Brian E. Small (T), Laura Erickson (B). XVI Brian E. Small. XVII Brian E. Small. XX–XXII Brian E. Small. XXIII Laura Erickson. XXIV Brian E. Small. XXIX Brian E. Small. XXV Brian E. Small. XXVII–XXVIII Brian E. Small. XXX–XXXI Brian E. Small. XXXI–XXXII Brian E. Small. XXXIV–XXXV Brian E. Small. 2–13 Brian E. Small. 14 Jacob Spendelow. 15–25 Brian E. Small. 26 Brian E. Small (T), Bob Steele (B). 27 Jacob Spendelow (T), Jim Zipp (B). 28–34 Brian E. Small. 35–36 Alan Murphy. 37–46 Brian E. Small. 47 Brian E. Small (T), Joe Fuhrman (B). 48–51 Brian E. Small. 52 Brian E. Small (L), Bob Steele (R). 53–62 Brian E. Small 63 Brian E. Small (L), Alan Murphy (R). 64 Brian E. Small 65 Alan Murphy (T), Brian E. Small (B). 66 Brian E. Small. 67 Brian E. Small (T), Jim Zipp (B). 68 Brian E. Small. 69 Jacob Spendelow (L), Jim Zipp (R). 70 Brian E. Small. 71 Alan Murphy (T), Brian E. Small (B). 72. Brian E. Small (L), Jacob Spendelow (R). 73–74 Jim Zipp. 75–89 Brian E. Small. 90 Brian E. Small (T), Mike Danzenbaker (B). 91 Brian E. Small (T), Mike Danzenbaker (B). 92–109 Brian E. Small. 110 Jim Zipp. 111–112 Brian E. Small. 113 Alan Murphy. 114–116 Brian E. Small. 117 Brian E. Small (T), Bob Steele (B). 118 Brian E. Small. 119 Brian E. Small (T), Laura Erickson (B). 120 Brian E. Small. 121 Reinhard Geisler. 122 Brian E. Small. 123 Brian E. Small (T), Alan Murphy (B). 124 Brian E. Small (T), A. Morris/VIREO (B). 125–138 Brian E. Small. 139 Jacob Spendelow. 140–141 Brian E. Small. 142 Jacob Spendelow. 143–145 Brian E. Small. 146 Brian E. Small (L), Alan Murphy (R). 147–148 Brian E. Small. 149 Brian E. Small (L), Laura Erickson (R). 150–152 Brian E. Small. 153 Brian E. Small (L), J. Schumacher/VIREO (R). 154 K. Smith/VIREO (L), Brian E. Small (R). 155 Brian E. Small. 156 Jim Zipp (T), Alan Murphy (B). 157 Brian E. Small (L), Bob Steele (R). 158–177 Brian E. Small. 178 Jim Zipp (L), Brian E. Small (R). 179–181 Brian E. Small. 182 Brian E. Small (L), Mike Danzenbaker (R). 183 Brian E. Small (L), Mike Danzenbaker (R). 184 Brian E. Small. 185 Bob Steele. 186–188 Brian E. Small. 189 Alan Murphy. 190–233 Brian E. Small. 234 Alan Murphy (T), Brian E. Small (B). 235–250 Brian E. Small. 251 Brian E. Small (T), Laura Erickson (B). 252–255 Brian E. Small. 256 Jacob Spendelow. 257–272 Brian E. Small. 273 Brian E. Small (T), Laura Erickson (B). 274–276 Brian E. Small. 277 Brian E. Small (T), Laura Erickson (B). 278–282 Brian E. Small. 283 Brian E. Small (T), Bob Steele (B). 284–302 Brian E. Small. 303 Jacob Spendelow (T), Brian E. Small (B). 304 Brian E. Small. 305 Alan Murphy. 306 Brian E. Small. 307 Brian E. Small (T), Laura Erickson (B). 308–310 Brian E. Small. 311 Brian E. Small (T), Laura Erickson (B). 312 Brian E. Small.

Checklist of the Birds of Minnesota

Regular (316 species)

- [ ] Greater White-fronted Goose
- [ ] Snow Goose
- [ ] Ross's Goose
- [ ] Cackling Goose
- [ ] Canada Goose
- [ ] Mute Swan
- [ ] Trumpeter Swan
- [ ] Tundra Swan
- [ ] Wood Duck
- [ ] Gadwall
- [ ] American Wigeon
- [ ] American Black Duck
- [ ] Mallard
- [ ] Blue-winged Teal
- [ ] Cinnamon Teal
- [ ] Northern Shoveler
- [ ] Northern Pintail
- [ ] Green-winged Teal
- [ ] Canvasback
- [ ] Redhead
- [ ] Ring-necked Duck
- [ ] Greater Scaup
- [ ] Lesser Scaup
- [ ] Harlequin Duck
- [ ] Surf Scoter
- [ ] White-winged Scoter
- [ ] Black Scoter
- [ ] Long-tailed Duck
- [ ] Bufflehead
- [ ] Common Goldeneye
- [ ] Barrow's Goldeneye
- [ ] Hooded Merganser
- [ ] Common Merganser
- [ ] Red-breasted Merganser
- [ ] Ruddy Duck
- [ ] Gray Partridge
- [ ] Ring-necked Pheasant
- [ ] Ruffed Grouse
- [ ] Spruce Grouse
- [ ] Sharp-tailed Grouse
- [ ] Greater Prairie-Chicken
- [ ] Wild Turkey
- [ ] Red-throated Loon
- [ ] Pacific Loon
- [ ] Common Loon
- [ ] Pied-billed Grebe
- [ ] Horned Grebe
- [ ] Red-necked Grebe
- [ ] Eared Grebe
- [ ] Western Grebe
- [ ] Clark's Grebe
- [ ] Double-crested Cormorant
- [ ] American White Pelican
- [ ] American Bittern
- [ ] Least Bittern
- [ ] Great Blue Heron
- [ ] Great Egret
- [ ] Snowy Egret
- [ ] Little Blue Heron
- [ ] Cattle Egret
- [ ] Green Heron
- [ ] Black-crowned Night-Heron
- [ ] Yellow-crowned Night-Heron
- [ ] White-faced Ibis
- [ ] Turkey Vulture
- [ ] Osprey
- [ ] Bald Eagle
- [ ] Northern Harrier
- [ ] Sharp-shinned Hawk
- [ ] Cooper's Hawk
- [ ] Northern Goshawk
- [ ] Red-shouldered Hawk
- [ ] Broad-winged Hawk
- [ ] Swainson's Hawk
- [ ] Red-tailed Hawk
- [ ] Rough-legged Hawk
- [ ] Golden Eagle
- [ ] Yellow Rail
- [ ] Virginia Rail
- [ ] Sora
- [ ] Common Gallinule
- [ ] American Coot
- [ ] Sandhill Crane
- [ ] American Avocet
- [ ] Black-bellied Plover
- [ ] American Golden-

Updated December 2014. Retrieved from http://moumn.org/Checklist_2014.pdf

Used with permission. Visit moumn.org for further information.

Plover
- [ ] Semipalmated Plover
- [ ] Piping Plover
- [ ] Killdeer
- [ ] Spotted Sandpiper
- [ ] Solitary Sandpiper
- [ ] Greater Yellowlegs
- [ ] Willet
- [ ] Lesser Yellowlegs
- [ ] Upland Sandpiper
- [ ] Whimbrel
- [ ] Hudsonian Godwit
- [ ] Marbled Godwit
- [ ] Ruddy Turnstone
- [ ] Red Knot
- [ ] Stilt Sandpiper
- [ ] Sanderling
- [ ] Dunlin
- [ ] Baird's Sandpiper
- [ ] Least Sandpiper
- [ ] White-rumped Sandpiper
- [ ] Buff-breasted Sandpiper
- [ ] Pectoral Sandpiper
- [ ] Semipalmated Sandpiper
- [ ] Short-billed Dowitcher
- [ ] Long-billed Dowitcher
- [ ] Wilson's Snipe
- [ ] American Woodcock
- [ ] Wilson's Phalarope
- [ ] Red-necked Phalarope
- [ ] Parasitic Jaeger
- [ ] Sabine's Gull
- [ ] Bonaparte's Gull
- [ ] Little Gull
- [ ] Franklin's Gull
- [ ] Ring-billed Gull

- [ ] Herring Gull
- [ ] Thayer's Gull
- [ ] Iceland Gull
- [ ] Lesser Black-backed Gull
- [ ] Glaucous Gull
- [ ] Great Black-backed Gull
- [ ] Caspian Tern
- [ ] Black Tern
- [ ] Common Tern
- [ ] Forster's Tern
- [ ] Rock Pigeon
- [ ] Eurasian Collared-Dove
- [ ] Mourning Dove
- [ ] Yellow-billed Cuckoo
- [ ] Black-billed Cuckoo
- [ ] Eastern Screech-Owl
- [ ] Great Horned Owl
- [ ] Snowy Owl
- [ ] Northern Hawk Owl
- [ ] Barred Owl
- [ ] Great Gray Owl
- [ ] Long-eared Owl
- [ ] Short-eared Owl
- [ ] Boreal Owl
- [ ] Northern Saw-whet Owl
- [ ] Common Nighthawk
- [ ] Eastern Whip-poor-will
- [ ] Chimney Swift
- [ ] Ruby-throated Hummingbird
- [ ] Belted Kingfisher
- [ ] Red-headed Woodpecker
- [ ] Red-bellied Woodpecker
- [ ] Yellow-bellied Sapsucker

- [ ] Downy Woodpecker
- [ ] Hairy Woodpecker
- [ ] American Three-toed Woodpecker
- [ ] Black-backed Woodpecker
- [ ] Northern Flicker
- [ ] Pileated Woodpecker
- [ ] American Kestrel
- [ ] Merlin
- [ ] Peregrine Falcon
- [ ] Prairie Falcon
- [ ] Olive-sided Flycatcher
- [ ] Eastern Wood-Pewee
- [ ] Yellow-bellied Flycatcher
- [ ] Acadian Flycatcher
- [ ] Alder Flycatcher
- [ ] Willow Flycatcher
- [ ] Least Flycatcher
- [ ] Eastern Phoebe
- [ ] Say's Phoebe
- [ ] Great Crested Flycatcher
- [ ] Western Kingbird
- [ ] Eastern Kingbird
- [ ] Loggerhead Shrike
- [ ] Northern Shrike
- [ ] Bell's Vireo
- [ ] Yellow-throated Vireo
- [ ] Blue-headed Vireo
- [ ] Warbling Vireo
- [ ] Philadelphia Vireo
- [ ] Red-eyed Vireo
- [ ] Canada Jay
- [ ] Blue Jay
- [ ] Black-billed Magpie
- [ ] American Crow
- [ ] Common Raven
- [ ] Horned Lark

- ☐ Purple Martin
- ☐ Tree Swallow
- ☐ Northern Rough-winged Swallow
- ☐ Bank Swallow
- ☐ Cliff Swallow
- ☐ Barn Swallow
- ☐ Black-capped Chickadee
- ☐ Boreal Chickadee
- ☐ Tufted Titmouse
- ☐ Red-breasted Nuthatch
- ☐ White-breasted Nuthatch
- ☐ Brown Creeper
- ☐ House Wren
- ☐ Winter Wren
- ☐ Sedge Wren
- ☐ Marsh Wren
- ☐ Carolina Wren
- ☐ Blue-gray Gnatcatcher
- ☐ Golden-crowned Kinglet
- ☐ Ruby-crowned Kinglet
- ☐ Eastern Bluebird
- ☐ Mountain Bluebird
- ☐ Townsend's Solitaire
- ☐ Veery
- ☐ Gray-cheeked Thrush
- ☐ Swainson's Thrush
- ☐ Hermit Thrush
- ☐ Wood Thrush
- ☐ American Robin
- ☐ Varied Thrush
- ☐ Gray Catbird
- ☐ Brown Thrasher
- ☐ Northern Mockingbird

- ☐ European Starling
- ☐ American Pipit
- ☐ Bohemian Waxwing
- ☐ Cedar Waxwing
- ☐ Lapland Longspur
- ☐ Chestnut-collared Longspur
- ☐ Smith's Longspur
- ☐ Snow Bunting
- ☐ Ovenbird
- ☐ Louisiana Waterthrush
- ☐ Northern Waterthrush
- ☐ Golden-winged Warbler
- ☐ Blue-winged Warbler
- ☐ Black-and-white Warbler
- ☐ Prothonotary Warbler
- ☐ Tennessee Warbler
- ☐ Orange-crowned Warbler
- ☐ Nashville Warbler
- ☐ Connecticut Warbler
- ☐ Mourning Warbler
- ☐ Kentucky Warbler
- ☐ Common Yellowthroat
- ☐ Hooded Warbler
- ☐ American Redstart
- ☐ Cape May Warbler
- ☐ Cerulean Warbler
- ☐ Northern Parula
- ☐ Magnolia Warbler
- ☐ Bay-breasted Warbler
- ☐ Blackburnian Warbler
- ☐ Yellow Warbler
- ☐ Chestnut-sided Warbler

- ☐ Blackpoll Warbler
- ☐ Black-throated Blue Warbler
- ☐ Palm Warbler
- ☐ Pine Warbler
- ☐ Yellow-rumped Warbler
- ☐ Black-throated Green Warbler
- ☐ Canada Warbler
- ☐ Wilson's Warbler
- ☐ Yellow-breasted Chat
- ☐ Spotted Towhee
- ☐ Eastern Towhee
- ☐ American Tree Sparrow
- ☐ Chipping Sparrow
- ☐ Clay-colored Sparrow
- ☐ Field Sparrow
- ☐ Vesper Sparrow
- ☐ Lark Sparrow
- ☐ Savannah Sparrow
- ☐ Grasshopper Sparrow
- ☐ Henslow's Sparrow
- ☐ Le Conte's Sparrow
- ☐ Nelson's Sparrow
- ☐ Fox Sparrow
- ☐ Song Sparrow
- ☐ Lincoln's Sparrow
- ☐ Swamp Sparrow
- ☐ White-throated Sparrow
- ☐ Harris's Sparrow
- ☐ White-crowned Sparrow
- ☐ Dark-eyed Junco
- ☐ Summer Tanager
- ☐ Scarlet Tanager
- ☐ Western Tanager
- ☐ Northern Cardinal

- [ ] Rose-breasted Grosbeak
- [ ] Blue Grosbeak
- [ ] Indigo Bunting
- [ ] Dickcissel
- [ ] Bobolink
- [ ] Red-winged Blackbird
- [ ] Eastern Meadowlark
- [ ] Western Meadowlark
- [ ] Yellow-headed Blackbird
- [ ] Rusty Blackbird
- [ ] Brewer's Blackbird
- [ ] Common Grackle
- [ ] Great-tailed Grackle
- [ ] Brown-headed Cowbird
- [ ] Orchard Oriole
- [ ] Baltimore Oriole
- [ ] Pine Grosbeak
- [ ] House Finch
- [ ] Purple Finch
- [ ] Red Crossbill
- [ ] White-winged Crossbill
- [ ] Common Redpoll
- [ ] Hoary Redpoll
- [ ] Pine Siskin
- [ ] American Goldfinch
- [ ] Evening Grosbeak
- [ ] House Sparrow

Casual (39 species)

- [ ] Black-bellied Whistling-Duck
- [ ] Brant
- [ ] Eurasian Wigeon
- [ ] King Eider
- [ ] Neotropic Cormorant
- [ ] Brown Pelican
- [ ] Glossy Ibis

- [ ] Black Vulture
- [ ] Mississippi Kite
- [ ] Ferruginous Hawk
- [ ] Black-necked Stilt
- [ ] Snowy Plover
- [ ] Ruff
- [ ] Purple Sandpiper
- [ ] Western Sandpiper
- [ ] Red Phalarope
- [ ] Pomarine Jaeger
- [ ] Black-legged Kittiwake
- [ ] Laughing Gull
- [ ] California Gull
- [ ] Slaty-backed Gull
- [ ] Arctic Tern
- [ ] White-winged Dove
- [ ] Burrowing Owl
- [ ] Gyrfalcon
- [ ] Scissor-tailed Flycatcher
- [ ] White-eyed Vireo
- [ ] Rock Wren
- [ ] Sprague's Pipit
- [ ] Worm-eating Warbler
- [ ] Yellow-throated Warbler
- [ ] Prairie Warbler
- [ ] Lark Bunting
- [ ] Golden-crowned Sparrow
- [ ] Black-headed Grosbeak
- [ ] Lazuli Bunting
- [ ] Painted Bunting
- [ ] Gray-crowned Rosy-Finch
- [ ] Eurasian Tree Sparrow

Accidental (81 species)

- [ ] Fulvous Whistling-

Duck
- [ ] Garganey
- [ ] Common Eider
- [ ] Smew
- [ ] Willow Ptarmigan
- [ ] Rock Ptarmigan
- [ ] Yellow-billed Loon
- [ ] Wood Stork
- [ ] Magnificent Frigatebird
- [ ] Tricolored Heron
- [ ] White Ibis
- [ ] Swallow-tailed Kite
- [ ] White-tailed Kite
- [ ] Black Rail
- [ ] King Rail
- [ ] Purple Gallinule
- [ ] Whooping Crane
- [ ] Wilson's Plover
- [ ] Long-billed Curlew
- [ ] Curlew Sandpiper
- [ ] Long-tailed Jaeger
- [ ] Dovekie
- [ ] Black Guillemot
- [ ] Long-billed Murrelet
- [ ] Ancient Murrelet
- [ ] Ivory Gull
- [ ] Black-headed Gull
- [ ] Ross's Gull
- [ ] Mew Gull
- [ ] Glaucous-winged Gull
- [ ] Least Tern
- [ ] Sandwich Tern
- [ ] Elegant Tern
- [ ] Band-tailed Pigeon
- [ ] Inca Dove
- [ ] Common Ground-Dove
- [ ] Groove-billed Ani
- [ ] Barn Owl

- [ ] Common Poorwill
- [ ] Chuck-will's-widow
- [ ] White-throated Swift
- [ ] Green Violetear
- [ ] Magnificent Hummingbird
- [ ] Anna's Hummingbird
- [ ] Costa's Hummingbird
- [ ] Rufous Hummingbird
- [ ] Calliope Hummingbird
- [ ] Lewis's Woodpecker
- [ ] Acorn Woodpecker
- [ ] Williamson's Sapsucker
- [ ] Crested Caracara
- [ ] Western Wood-Pewee
- [ ] Vermilion Flycatcher
- [ ] Ash-throated Flycatcher
- [ ] Tropical/Couch's Kingbird
- [ ] Cassin's Kingbird
- [ ] Fork-tailed Flycatcher
- [ ] Clark's Nutcracker
- [ ] Violet-green Swallow
- [ ] Pygmy Nuthatch
- [ ] Bewick's Wren
- [ ] American Dipper
- [ ] Northern Wheatear
- [ ] Fieldfare
- [ ] Curve-billed Thrasher
- [ ] Sage Thrasher
- [ ] McCown's Longspur
- [ ] MacGillivray's Warbler
- [ ] Kirtland's Warbler

- [ ] Black-throated Gray Warbler
- [ ] Townsend's Warbler
- [ ] Hermit Warbler
- [ ] Painted Redstart
- [ ] Green-tailed Towhee
- [ ] Brewer's Sparrow
- [ ] Black-throated Sparrow
- [ ] Baird's Sparrow
- [ ] Bullock's Oriole
- [ ] Scott's Oriole
- [ ] Brambling
- [ ] Cassin's Finch

Extirpated (2 species)

- [ ] Northern Bobwhite
- [ ] Eskimo Curlew

Extinct (1 species)

- [ ] Passenger Pigeon

Species Index

Laura Erickson, 2014 recipient of the American Birding Association's Roger Tory Peterson Award and author of eight previous books about birds, has been a teacher, wildlife rehabilitator, public speaker, and science editor at the Cornell Lab of Ornithology. She is a contributing editor for *BirdWatching* magazine. Since 1986, she has been producing the "For the Birds" radio program that airs on many radio stations and is available as a podcast on iTunes. She lives in Duluth, Minnesota, with her husband and little birding dog Pip.

Brian E. Small is a full-time professional bird and nature photographer. For more than 30 years, he has traveled widely across North America to capture images of birds in their native habitats. He served as the photo editor at *Birding* magazine for 15 years. Small grew up in Los Angeles, graduated from U.C.L.A. in 1982 and still lives there today with his wife Ana, daughter Nicole, and son Tyler.

Quick Index

See the Species Index for a complete listing of all the birds in the *American Birding Association Field Guide to Birds of Minnesota*.